Hunting in America

HUNTING

by Charles F. Waterman | A Ridge Press Book

ᵀⁿAMERICA

Holt, Rinehart and Winston | New York

Editor-in-Chief: Jerry Mason
Editor: Adolph Suehsdorf
Art Director: Albert Squillace
Associate Editor: Moira Duggan
Associate Editor: Barbara Hoffbeck
Art Associate: Mark Liebergall
Art Associate: David Namias
Art Production: Doris Mullane

Published in the United States of America in 1973 by Holt, Rinehart and
Winston, Inc., Publishers, 383 Madison Avenue, New York, New York 10017, U.S.A.
Published simultaneously in Canada by Holt, Rinehart and Winston of Canada, Limited.
Waterman, Charles F
     Hunting in America.
     "A Ridge Press book."
     1. Hunting—North America—History. I. Title.
SK40.W37   799.2'97   73-78306
ISBN 0-03-010721-0
Printed and bound in Italy by Mondadori Editore, Verona.

To my wife Debie.

Contents

Foreword

*Compiling a history of American hunting is
hunting in itself. The prehistoric era is recorded in shreds of
archaeological fact and clothed in romantic supposition.
Only as later hunters made their own records did the narrative
become more factual and substantial.*

❧

*The earliest written accounts of hunting were
incidental to other reporting; there may be one sentence on
hunting in the entire account of an early
settlement or expedition. It was not until the nineteenth century
that hunters and travelers began to set down their
experiences with game in a comprehensive and orderly manner.
The beaver and buffalo were especially
well recorded, since these animals were bases
of economy and factors in settlement, exploration, and politics.*

❧

*As the kill of game species reached alarming
numbers in the last years of the nineteenth century, there came*

the first tentative action toward protection

and management on the part of naturalists and concerned sportsmen.

During the past half-century, as the number

of hunters increased and game management, of necessity, became

a well-applied science, the literature

of the history of hunting in America came forth in volumes

rather than casual paragraphs.

In putting this material together I am especially

indebted for their help to librarians like Mrs. Chester Coons, who

always knew where "there might be something,"

even if it meant searching for mentions on scattered and brittle

pages; to naturalists like Walter Kenner,

who wonders about the why of everything; to hunting authorities

like Leighton Baker, who mercilessly separates

fact from fiction; and to photographers like Bill Browning,

who saw no reason why a Sharps rifle and

a buffalo could not be photographed together in 1972.

Charles F. Waterman
April, 1973

1. The Land

Primeval

Twelve thousand years ago there were scattered bands of buffalo grazing on the Great Plains of what is now Kansas. With them were herds of camels, wild horses, and antelope. Some of the bison were giants, with horns that spread six feet, and the men who hunted them followed like furtive guerrilla fighters, watching from folds in the landscape, and waiting patiently for the strayed calf or the tired old bull unable to compete with younger animals. They would attack at the signal of their leader, the best hunter of the clan. For the spearmen in the ravine, big-game hunting was a form of warfare, a battle fought on even terms.

Man was not alone on the perimeter of the buffalo herds, for there were giant wolves on the prairies. In the timbered foothills were great bears, and the saber-toothed cats hunted both man and his quarry. The trail behind had to be watched as closely as the track ahead.

Big as they were, the bison and carnivores were dwarfed by the American elephants and near-elephants: the hairy mammoth that stayed close to the retreating ice; the imperial mammoth that stood more than thirteen feet at the shoulder, carried sixteen-foot tusks, and grazed on the western plains; and the flat-skulled mastodon that lived from Alaska to Florida.

Mammoths and mastodons were in the category of the buffalo—dangerous to the hunter, but desirable game. In warm weather the hunters' camps were made beside such big kills. In winter, when meat kept well, it was taken to shelter, usually a cave, for man was growing more able in the cooking and drying of the meat he gained through his exploits.

The ice was retreating to the North, as it still retreats, at a pace measured in centuries. It was escorted by a strip of tundra extending across the continent and was followed by the ancestors of today's caribou and musk ox.

At one time, abound 18,000 B.C., the ice sheath had reached as far south as what is now Kansas City and drew up most of the world's water. In its vastness, it covered Canada and the northern United States and reached from Alaska to Siberia, creating a land bridge between the North American and Asiatic continents. As the weather moderated, the ice thawed and receded.

On a spring morning 12,000 years ago, the Great Plains probably appeared much as they did later to the first explorers, except that there was more water. There were wider marshes and more lakes, and thick grama grasses, with just enough break to the land to afford shelter from storms. It was well-stocked, almost perfect big-game country.

Many of the antelope species present were later to become extinct, but among them were the ancestors of the pronghorn, not very different from the contemporary animal. The hunter who followed the watercourses and ravines could not always depend on large game, and he found rabbits and reptiles between times of plenty. In spring there were nesting birds, and when he hunted near hills and forests he could find the slow-witted opossum or porcupine, both of which have survived while swifter and probably more intelligent creatures have disappeared.

Some North American horses were the size of dogs; another type, known in Texas, weighed more than a ton. The earliest American men knew horses as game rather than as servants. They were most plentiful on the plains, and the most common form, running in great herds, was near the size of a modern animal. But 12,000 years ago, horses were soon to dis-

Opening pages: America's
primeval wilderness was a varied sweep of forest,
mountain, valley, and swamp
continually recreated by ice, heat,
and evolution. This contemporary Yukon vista
is an image of the past, a
wildlife habitat providing bog and meadow
for moose, timbered slopes
for bear, and high ridges for the wild sheep.

appear from the continent, brought to extinction by factors that are as yet unknown. A different kind of horse returned to America with the Spaniards, to prove one of the hardiest of wild animals, as well as the most valued beast of burden of all time.

As the Ice Age progressed, American camels began to disappear. Traffic over the land bridge to Asia undoubtedly went two ways; the camels may have gone from East to West and become progenitors of Asiatic species. Only a few of the tribe stayed in South America, represented today by the llama and vicuna.

A giant ground sloth, weighing more than 1,500 pounds, browsed on branches twenty feet high and walked ponderously on long-clawed feet, shaped for hanging from branches which the monster had become too heavy to climb. It lived in much of the South and probably elsewhere. As it pruned the leaves it braced itself with an enormous blunt tail. It may have been a windfall for the early hunters, but such an ungainly mountain of meat was a blind alley of evolution; only the sloths that moved in the trees survived—and they in South America.

Today's peccaries of the Southwest were preceded by other species, some of them much larger, and at least one was a more advanced form, having heavier and longer legs than the little pigs that survived. Some carnivores—minks, weasels, martens, skunks, otters, badgers, wolverines, raccoons, foxes, wolves, and pumas—have not changed greatly since the time the ground sloth died.

When the hunters watched the bison 12,000 years ago, the saber-toothed tiger still lived, although he was almost outdated. Largest of the sword-toothed cats, he stood the height of a leopard, but was much heavier in body and legs and had a short tail. His eight-inch fangs were stabbers and slashers rather than biters. They were capable of piercing the hide of a mammoth or holding a writhing smaller prey. He was perhaps the most fearsome beast of his time, but his fangs had developed too far and it was difficult for him to chew anything but great chunks of meat; it may have been that in time the tiger starved. Remains of many of them were found in the Los Angeles tar pits, a bog of oozing petroleum, where the tigers became mired beside their quarry while vultures with twelve-foot wingspread shrieked in excitement overhead.

Among the ancestors of living bears, extinction had come to some species, including cave bears, but there were still large bears that resembled the grizzly of much later, to be avoided as the sabertooth was.

There are theories that the disappearance of the larger animals was a matter of evolution that favored smaller creatures; it is also thought that man's predation played a part. There were numerous climatic changes about the time the giants died. They may have been unable to adapt to extreme fluctuations in temperature, and may have lacked the instinct to migrate when the life zones in which they flourished moved north or south, away from them.

Of the North American big-game animals living today, many are directly traceable to Asiatic ancestry, evidently having crossed the land bridge between Alaska and Siberia. Wild sheep came across the bridge, extending their belt of residence in high places of the world from the Mediterranean to what is now Mexico; they did not cross the isthmus into South America. The white Dall sheep of Alaska, possibly the last of those arrivals, may now be merging with the bighorn to the South, perhaps an observable evolutionary change in our own time. The Dall is nearly pure white, but the

*Man met his environment as
hunter and hunted, emerging from the
safety of rocky caves to
fight great beasts with crude weapons.
The hairy mammoth lived in
snow and ice; caribou and reindeer
would survive him.
Glacier and heat carved the mountains,
dug the lakes, regulated
weather throughout the ages.*

*Mammoths died in natural bogs
or in prepared pits, where puny men slew them
with multiple blows, living
near the carcass until it was consumed.
The slope-browed mastodon and the
saber-toothed tiger roamed the same range as
enemies; both vanished as the
glaciers melted, the Earth changed, and more
adaptable animals appeared.*

Stone sheep to the south of it may range from white to dark brown or black, and its horn structure more closely resembles that of the bighorn, which resides still farther south. Some observers believe the Stone sheep is a phase between the Dall and the bighorn, and that it is a product of interbreeding.

Although the Rocky Mountain goat must have descended from travelers of the bridge and has a relationship with the chamois, it is unique, without close relatives, and it seems to have lived through much of the Ice Age. There is a theory that the goat survived, even lonelier than it is today, living above the terrible sheets of ice where the bare peaks, scoured by cold winds, supported the skimpy vegetation it prefers.

America's very first hunters must have entered the continent over the land bridge at what is now Bering Strait—a bridge that changed in size with the centuries and may have existed intermittently. Between about 25,000 and 9,000 B.C., the connection was a wide plain.

The first hunters are the ghosts of prehistory. They left little mark on the land—no structures, no graves, no traceable thread of human progress. Like the mountain trappers of thousands of years later, they moved across America with the game they sought, and their numbers cannot be guessed. They are known mainly through the tools they left, tools of hunting that remain with the bones of mammoths and ancient camels long extinct, and their own bones are so scarce as to provide more questions than answers. Out of necessity, archaeologists must try to outline their history by analyzing the stone spear points that are the most numerous relics of these hunters.

The first American hunters were much like modern man, without the outsized eyeteeth that their primitive ancestors had used as weapons. Few archaeologists will concede that the first American men could have arrived earlier than 20,000 years ago. They must have been armed with hunting tools, and they advanced probably in small parties or family groups. They went in short moves, as quarry was trailed or chased, or as suitable shelter was sighted up ahead. Their advance carried them, nevertheless, the length of two continents, and they reached the southern tip of South America, probably over many generations. However long it took, the early hunters scattered widely, and at the time Europeans arrived in America—a scant five hundred years ago —it is estimated that there were 2,200 western-hemisphere languages, more than those of the rest of the world combined.

The more primitive a culture the more nearly its instruments blend with the formations of nature, for the earliest people did little forming themselves, utilizing instead stones or sticks that were already tool-shaped. While the spear and arrow points of later hunters tell something of their users, there is doubt among archaeologists as to the remains of the conjectured "pebble cultures" found along old stream beds where the first men must have walked and camped. What can be inferred from a stone that seems unusually fitted to a hand and suited for scraping? Or one that might have been sharpened for cutting or piercing? Both could be accidents of nature. In Africa, there are pebble tools believed to have been employed more than two million years ago; but American pebble shapings are still questioned.

Stones and sticks were the first weapons, and then came the sharpened stick—later hardened in the fire which man had partly mastered, then a short spear with claw or horn tip, followed by the chipped-stone point. The throwing board, or atlatl, de-

Rivers and marshes cradled
much of America's wildlife and were both
obstacles and highways for
early man and his game. The giant ground sloth,
an awkward mountain of flesh,
outgrew tree branches and was helpless
against man. The dog—first
of the domestic animals— helped heroically
in the hunt, harried bison for Indians.

Primitive man conquered wild
animals when he learned to make tools—at
first simple weapons from
appropriately shaped stones, then clubs, spears,
and arrows. His materials
included parts of the game he killed. He made
fire an ally, and his family
groups increased from sparse bands of hunters
to tribes and nations.

veloped before the bow. It was a notched stick that accepted the butt of a spear shaft and gave the hunter additional leverage as he supported and guided the missile with one hand and threw it with the other. Even after the bow was developed, the atlatl served with it, and the short spear it hurled was better than a flimsy reed arrow for hand-to-fang combat. For small game, bolas were made with stone or bone weights attached at either end of a thong. At close range, they were capable of entangling and bringing down even a flying bird.

Burial places and complex tombs filled with artifacts were not found with the earliest hunting weapons, for burials would have been a frivolous custom in an existence tied only to the trail ahead and the guarded track behind. American archaeologists have had to depend on random finds to reveal the life of hunters in North America more than 4,000 years ago. The famous Clovis, Folsom, and Sandia points, well-formed for spear shafts, were discovered in the Southwest, but there is much disagreement as to their dating. The Clovis points have been dated to 9,200 B.C., the Folsom points to 9,000-8,000 B.C., and the Sandia points farther back, by some accounts. The points thought to be earlier are heavier than the later ones, probably for use against the giant beasts that were beginning to die out at the retreat of the glaciers which closed the Pleistocene epoch around 9,000 B.C. Prior to that time, game was plentiful, found in herds comparable to those of the Serengeti, but the huge animals were beginning to disappear. The true purge began about 11,000 years ago.

Some of the ancient spear and arrow points were designed in forms unsurpassed by modern craftsmen. Those first hunters learned skills unsuspected for a time by archaeologists. It was once believed, for instance, that the construction of a spear point was a task of many hours of chipping, but a modern craftsman, developing his own "primitive" methods, found that a good point was a matter of only a few minutes' work and that pressure chipping could be executed with materials softer than the point itself.

So the hunter might make his points during a brief rest stop, or while he sat by a fire, and he must have made some of them while he watched for game, for the seeker of arrowheads finds flakes and broken points on logical outcroppings that would have given a good view of game trails below. The perfect points are not likely to be there, however, for the workman who fashioned them took them along, or fired them at passing targets, leaving the scraps of his labors strewn on hundreds of mountain overlooks across the length and breadth of the continent.

Even 10,000 or 12,000 years ago, some of the points were fluted, evidently so that a handle could be better attached, and the contours that resulted from skillful chipping of flint or agate had cutting qualities unmatched even by modern steel arrowheads. Some modern points are shaped in frank imitation of those used by the skin-clad stalkers of thousands of years ago.

It was about the time that the bow and arrow were developed that domestic dogs must have begun to aid American hunters. It is uncertain just when dog and wolf divided from their common source. In parts of the undeveloped world today there are wild dogs, not considered wolves but having wolf habits. And modern dogs often revert to the wild when neglected.

The dog family descended from a wolf-like animal, *Tomarctus*, which lived some fifteen million years ago, and even the fireside pet is but little removed from his resourceful wild relatives. He can reject man if necessary for survival.

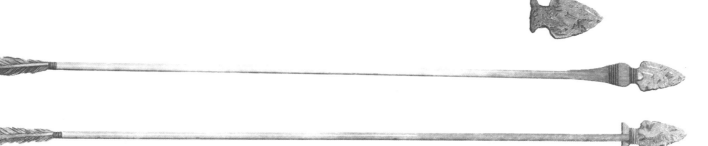

The dog's role rose and fell with the fortunes of some of the plains Indians. Dogs pulled the travois, or were equipped with packsaddles. The Spaniards found western Indians using long strings of dogs with packs, as many as five hundred in some trains, with loads of up to thirty pounds for "medium-sized dogs." After the plains Indians acquired horses, the dog's status seemed to change and the "half-starved" canine was often part of the later Indian camp. When buffalo hunting was under way, dogs were fat and horses lean. When a permanent camp was established for winter or for a rest from travel, dogs were forced to live largely on the game they could catch for themselves, and it was the horses that prospered on grass selected before the camp was set.

In early digging by archaeologists it was hard to tell whether dogs had actually been living with men, or if they had been used for meat, or if the association was accidental. After the dog's domestication, there was a notable change in the animal's diet. It happened as man began cooking in containers. Since this took most of the nourishment from the bones of larger animals, the dogs began a diet of smaller creatures, especially fish. In modern times Eskimo dogs have been able to live almost entirely on fish for long periods.

There is an eerie element in the modern relationship between dogs and coyotes, which will hunt and kill each other but sometimes interbreed to

*Dall rams, northernmost
American wild sheep, rest on Alaska
mountainside where escape
routes border their steep pastures and
cold, snow-fed brooks. Above:
Early artist depicts sheep in leaping
flight, while calm goats survey
world from ledge. Bull elk was dramatic
sight for first travelers.*

produce the coydog. The hunting dog after birds meets the coyote face to face and they study each other in silence and quietly turn away. The hunter who has seen this happen feels he has brushed against a distant past, a past that has somehow brought him to his present sport.

By the time the men in the ravines and behind the low hills watched their plains game some 12,000 years ago, the long evolutionary journey was well advanced and the bridge to Asia was sinking into the cold and misty currents of Bering Strait.

By then fire was both weapon and comfort, and man could drive game with it. Herds of plains grazers moved before creeping lines of fire and then closed behind them to consume the bright new growth that sprang up. In the forests, sections of mature timber were razed to make way for new successions.

While many of the creatures of the Stone Age died out, Stone Age man did not. Surprisingly, he can still be studied firsthand. In the twentieth century there are some 250,000 primitive hunters still living. They belong to scattered tribes in the wildernesses of Africa, Asia, and South America. More are discovered from time to time, as in Mindanao, in the Philippines, where a handful of Tasadays, termed Stone Age men, was found living in caves in 1972. There must have been hunting cultures that died out completely, and others that retrogressed, or were completely untouched, as the world changed.

The hunters on the perimeter of the bison herd were ambushers and not trackers. They had moved with the game in a series of camps made where animals had fallen. There were only a dozen men, followed at a distance by women and children, and although they had seen some ravines into which buffalo might be stampeded, they had not attempted a drive for they might lose contact with the main herd by frightening it. Meat could not be kept for long in summer, so they lived from day to day. When the bison were too cautious, there were sometimes deer to be had in the willowed draws or rabbits in their sheltered forms along the banks.

They kept downwind from the bison, following the slow travel of the grazing animals. Meanwhile they watched bands of antelope drifting on grassy slopes—for the early hunters were opportunists. They were attentive, too, to the waterholes they found in the shallow ravines, especially those with trampled borders and well-marked trails leading in from the prairie. The tracks of the buffalo were thick and among them were the lighter hoofmarks of antelope, horses, and deer. The men made mental notes of any waterhole that seemed boggy, a ready-made trap for a flustered or wounded animal, and it was from the crest of a small hill that they saw the mammoth.

Of all the North American elephants, only the imperial mammoth could have been so large, huge even in the immensity of grass and sky. More than thirteen feet at the shoulder, as large as the African tusker of a later day, the mammoth lived on the plains west of the Mississippi. Unlike the flat-skulled and shorter-legged mastodon, persistent remnant of an earlier time, the imperial mammoth had a high-crowned head, almost peaked, and its long back sloped steeply from enormous shoulders. Its tusks turned upward and backward with age and might have measured as much as sixteen feet. In their sweeping curves, they were becoming useless ornaments, of a weight totaling almost a thousand pounds.

The bull had moved away from its small herd of associates and ambled toward the watercourse, an exercise in patience for the watchers, but they were men who lived largely by waiting and they were silent in alders and willows, having taken their positions with a minimum of communication.

The mammoth shuffled in a loose gait, taking an occasional twist of grass in its trunk, and as it neared the willow border its 12,000 pounds made ground tremors that must have been easily felt by tense men crouching against damp earth.

The hunters launched their attack, thrusting their spears up from almost beneath the enormous creature, aiming not for the heart or lungs, but for the belly where internal bleeding would bring inexorable death. The cutting blades were broad and triangular, their edges scalloped in outsized sawteeth by the natural chipping of the flint, and they went deep as they came upward, driven with the strength of legs and back as the hunters rose from a squatting position. One of the spears did not come out easily and its owner let it go and leaped with his companions to safety as their prey thundered off with writhing trunk and a surprised bellow, not yet feeling the drain of the spearhead that worked deeper with his movements. Such a heavy animal could not be killed quickly with spears except by a lucky thrust to a nerve center.

The trail was bloody at first, easily followed by the hunters, and many hours after the blood had stopped it became a stumbling route, first across the open grassland, and then inevitably turning toward water as nearly all wounded animals will do. Finally, with night approaching, the beast came near the edge of another stream with its pursuers close behind. It saw the hunters and moved away clumsily, without drinking, to go on to the edge of a marshy river. This time the men did not drive it away but circled cautiously, and when the mammoth was above his knees in mud and water they charged noisily. The animal plunged deeper, unable to withdraw from the bog. Even then, death was a long while coming, but the result was assured. When their quarry was helpless, the men scrambled on its back and drove spears into the spine near the great head. Centuries later the points were found, hard and sharp among the bones of their victim.

If preservation had been possible, the meat of one such mammoth could have fed a party of thirty hunters for an entire summer. But many of the kills were mired in swamp, almost covered by water, and the butchering was crude and incomplete, with most of the animal left to residents of the mud and water.

While the meat was good, such a fallen giant would be basis of a camp, provided competition for it was not too great. Sensitive wolf noses would trace the kill from another valley, and the gray wolf shadows would slip silently through the grass by day. At night, their eyes would gleam about the fire and their howls rise as those of their descendants do when there is a fresh kill. The giant dire wolf is long gone but other gray wolves of prairie and forest lived after him.

As the mammoths and mastodons dwindled, man was already becoming expert in mass hunting, and soon the impromptu buffalo cliff would be more carefully chosen; there would be scarecrows and even fences to funnel game to its death. The bow and arrow would extend the flint point's range, and the cave deposits would one day show that man boiled his meat and fed scraps to his dog. The hunters have used many of the same caves for 10,000 years, with stone scrapers far down in the detritus and the modern rifleman's discarded bean can at the top.

2. The Red

Hunter

few years before Columbus' epic voyage, in a wilderness later to be known as New York State, some Indians carefully apply a torch to the forest floor. They have chosen a day when the breeze will carry the flames away from their village. The ground cover was burned the year before and the year before that, and there is no danger of damaging the large oaks or pines. The fire curls through the grass at moderate speed and rabbits hop away when it blazes high at the brushy spots where they have been resting. Still, there is no panic, for a hundred generations of cottontail rabbits have moved before such fires, sometimes rounding the end of the fire line, sometimes moving on to a brook where the flames will falter and die.

The whitetail deer move before the fire, too, in no great hurry. They take advantage of any bushy cover for, although evening is coming on, it is still daylight. When the deer reach the brook by a roundabout route, they are well ahead of the fire and they pause before showing themselves in the open. They have traveled by a series of brisk moves in the open places and have stopped each time before leaving cover to inspect the unsheltered space for enemies. At the brook they cross and disappear almost instantly into the thick, green swamp where they will bed until nightfall. The fire will not follow them there.

Not all wildlife retreats from the fire. The blaze started well back in a forested area and moved out of the trees and into open parks at intervals, the smoke rising as a trace of haze at first, and becoming thicker as the light breeze fails to clear it thoroughly behind the busy fire line. A number of songbirds have appeared in the wake of the fire, even before the burn has cooled, looking for exposed beetles or grasshoppers. In the upper edge of the gauzy smoke curtain a sharp-shinned hawk glides, watching for the movement of a field mouse. A sparrow hawk hovers in search of insects. The fire has revealed many secrets of the grassy areas.

At the approach of evening the air becomes more humid, as the Indians knew it would. The ground cools and other insect hunters—a band of wild turkeys—are busy in the burned areas. A watching hunter marks their progress, knowing they will roost nearby, going up into trees with a noisy flapping of wings at a spot where he will find them again at dawn.

In only a few days the blackened ground will send forth green shoots and deer will take advantage of the tender growth and of the minerals made available by the fire. The burn has protected the Indians' village from the threat of an uncontrolled blaze. Now it has become a baited trap, for as the deer move about it at dusk, bowmen wait in ambush.

The red man helped to make the eastern forest what it was and what it became. He had no master plan, but in effect he created a woodland hospitable to flocks of wild turkey and herds of whitetail deer. He did this through the use of fire, opening areas of the forest floor to sunlight and to low second-growth vegetation in which a variety of wildlife could thrive. The first game to appear after the fire came for the insects and small burrowing creatures that were burned or left unprotected by the flames, then for the new green shoots and minerals found in the blackened wake of the fire. Thereafter, for more than a decade, the path of the fire would produce a succession of plants especially attractive to browsers and grazers, and there would be berries and buds for ruffed grouse.

Fire also was the Indian's method of clearing forest areas for his villages and eliminating

*Opening pages: Early Indian
hunter shaped flint to make arrowheads that were
superior to modern steel ones.
Bone, wood, sinew, and claws all became parts
of Indian weapons. The bow
was a descendant of the throwing stick, or
atlatl. Indian archers varied
greatly in ability and equipment. Eskimo hunters
invented finest weapons.*

underbrush that could be an incendiary hazard if lightning struck. He even used fire to drive game toward trap and hunter. He used it in the Appalachians, where grassy balds were specked with game, and he used it, with less pronounced effect, in the Sierras and the Rockies, where elk herds left their shadowed bedding grounds to feed in wide parks. If the Indian neglected his duty for a time, or if nature delayed the lightning bolts too long, the wildfire—when it did come—would build on luxuriant ground cover to a roaring, crashing horror with all life fleeing before it. At such times a part of the forest was destroyed rather than enhanced.

To the first white explorers the forests along the eastern seaboard and inland across the Appalachians appeared dense and impenetrable. In actuality they were broken and varied stands of trees, grassy, gladed timberlands, scattered prairies and savannas, and thick but interrupted swamps. Such forests generally appear unbroken from their peripheries.

The eastern forest ran along the Atlantic Coast from northern Maine to the Florida Everglades, and inland past the Appalachians to the beginnings of the midwestern prairies. Throughout it were scattered settlements of forest Indians, living in wigwam villages they moved frequently to fit the patterns of forest game. Villages were considerably separated, but the Indian population was possibly near the limit that could be comfortably accommodated, for hunting Indians require a range to match the game's.

In 1600 the Indians found plentiful deer and turkey, residents of the edges—the margins of thick swamps, the boundaries of rocky slopes, the borders of thickets, in general, the places where the woods were free of matted undergrowth. Many of these borders were the result of fire, either controlled or wild.

The white man greatly feared fire, since his settlements were more permanent than the Indian's, and this fear led to the unnatural suppression of a natural process. Whereas the red man used fire to create game habitats for future years, the white man cleared the land with axe and saw; it was three centuries before he learned the sound fire procedures of the Indian.

Between the time of the red man's empire and the contemporary world of industry, the land has changed and rechanged. The deer and turkey have come and gone with the changes, but now their times of plenty can be promised and their eventual scarcity predicted, if not prevented.

In the Northeast, the splayed tracks of the moose in the shallow snow were followed by the relentless webbed trail of Algonkin snowshoes. Eventually, vaguely frightened by the pursuit, the moose might abandon his caution and enter a drifted area, where, after breaking through the crust, even his great legs could not find firm footing in deep, fluffy snow. For the pursuing Indian the trail might be long, but he risked starving if he left it. Patience was the deadliest of the primitive hunter's weapons.

The Indian lived close to his game, substituting superior cunning for the hawk's piercing sight, the deer's acute hearing, and the bear's sensitive nose. With even the crudest of weapons he could be a successful hunter, and he used camouflage and disguise as well as decoys.

The aboriginal hunter was of necessity an opportunist. The cries of hunting wolves were a signal to Indians who might be able to intercept the chase and kill an animal already exhausted by the gray pursuers. Indians of mountain country watched for snowslides that might mean entrapped and frozen game,

Fire serves the forest,
opening ground to new growth and
curbing progress of
underbrush that can fuel even more
devastating conflagration.
Whitetail buck lives on edges of
forest. Most adaptable of
all big game, he is close neighbor
of man from coast to coast.

and in buffalo country they gathered meat from the spring thaw as buffalo were washed down the rivers after being captured by flood or after breaking through rotting ice.

In their various locales the Indians depended on different game species. Plains Indians developed a buffalo culture, forest Indians collected a wide variety of game, and some Pacific Coast tribes relied on the salmon runs. But for nearly all of these peoples the deer was a staple food, filling in when other game was scarce. For many tribes the deer was also a primary source of shelter materials and tools. Small enough to be transported by one or two men, large enough to furnish days of food, and fragile enough to be felled by a modestly powered bow, the deer kept the red man alive.

Elk, moose, and caribou are members of the deer family, but they are relatively recent arrivals from the Old World. It is the whitetail, blacktail, and mule deer the American refers to when he speaks of deer, and they are of such long residence in North America that their beginnings are lost millions of years in the past. Highly adaptable, deer have withstood changes in climate and land that destroyed other game. When white men began to change the continent, there were an estimated fifty million of them.

The mule deer and its near relative, the blacktail, have always lived west of the Mississippi, the blacktail only near the Pacific Coast. But the whitetail has covered the contiguous United States, adapting to divergent habitats. There are 400-pound whitetails in Maine; the miniature Florida Keys deer are the size of a dog. In the Southwest the little Coues whitetail is the flick of a white flag at edge of the desert, and in the Deep South the swamp whitetail spends much of its time in several inches of water. Where the Indian went there

were nearly always deer to help sustain life.

As a vital part of existence, the deer entered legend, religion, and ceremony. There were antler headdresses, much like those employing buffalo horns. Mound Builders of the Mississippi Valley left deer bones in their refuse heaps and the effigy mounds of the Great Lakes area were sometimes shaped in the form of deer. There were many deer bones in New England kitchen middens and Aztec manuscripts in Mexico were written on deerskin.

Terrain dictated the Indians' methods of hunting deer. Canoe Indians of the Northeast killed much of their game in the water. It was common to organize a deer drive that pushed whitetails to a promontory extending into a river or lake, and when the game plunged into the water it was pursued by waiting canoemen. A deer swims swiftly, and drawing abreast of it with a single canoe is not simple, for the animal will alter course so quickly that only an adroit paddle man can follow. The deer swims low in the water, offering a small target of head and neck, but there were athletes who could leave a canoe and make a kill with a knife.

Canoe hunters frequently intercepted deer or moose making voluntary crossings of deep water. With moose feeding on a lake or river bottom, they used their craft with deadly effect. The silent canoe approached shore, the paddler still when the animal's head was up, moving quickly when it was submerged to feed. Unused to danger from seaward, the moose might pay little attention to his floating enemies until they were within arm's length.

At night the canoe was used with a torch in the bow. Drinking deer stood transfixed, awaiting the arrow. Animals surprised by lights sometimes became confused by their own leaping shadows and

Birchbark canoe was way
of life for Indians of Northeast, who used it
both for travel and for hunting. It
allowed large game to be driven into deep
water and bowman or spearman
to approach closely and quietly for death thrust.
Following pages: Bald eagle
became symbol of power to Indian because of its
majestic flight and sharp eyesight.

might flee in the direction of the bowman.

The birchbark canoe was swift. It could be propelled by a single man in the water and carried by him on the trail. And it offered dry-land shelter. It made highways of rivers and lakes, and knitted the eastern wilderness together. Centuries after the birchbark canoe was developed, when the buckskin shirt had given way to calico and nearly all Indians had forsaken the birchbark skills, white artisans studied the graceful lines and purposeful lashings and could find no improvement for the red man's work.

Indian hunters of the plains often dressed in deerskins to approach herded mule deer, a ruse that worked best in late fall when game was distracted by the rut. Choosing an area where harems of does and belligerent bucks were scattered loosely, the hunters could come upwind with sunlight behind them, appearing only as other deer and attracting scant notice from an animal with only fair eyesight. Short sticks were sometimes used to increase the deception, the patient huntsman using them as forelegs while his short bow was held in readiness. A possessive muley buck might even come to meet such an apparition if the cover were suitable, and the arrow's range might be feet instead of rods. If the arrow did not kill immediately, it was no matter, for a hunter who could follow a healthy deer's trail for miles without snow found little difficulty with the stumbling, bloodstained track of dying quarry.

There were gray wolves about the edges of the buffalo bands, attentive and patient escorts for the sick, aged, or very young. Healthy adults paid them little attention, and an Indian on all fours, carefully covered by a wolf's skin, could work near to a herd and then make a sudden rush into its midst, perhaps even passing guardian bulls on the fringes to reach the concentration of vulnerable cows and calves.

There was another method, in which hunters disguised by buffalo or deer skins served as decoys, taking a resolute lead as a nervous herd milled uncertainly and then followed what appeared to be an animal that knew the way to safety. The route could lead to a deadly cliff, a well-planned ambush, or a stockade. Where nature had not provided a trap, the Indians—and, farther north, the Eskimos—had learned to build their own. There were log, stone, and brush impoundments of triangular shape with wing fences that diverted the animals to a narrow gap leading to a tighter enclosure. Here they were forced into such close quarters they could easily be speared. At a distance from the trap, only crude wing fences were needed, and a few scattered hunters were enough to keep the herd moving, even though the barriers could have been breached at any point. Once heavy animals were enclosed in an impoundment, sharpened stakes projecting from the walls kept them from breaking out.

The pronghorn of the plains was unable to use its speed once it entered an impoundment and was unlikely to jump out because of some perverse quirk of nature which prevents it from making high leaps, although it will jump shadows and is capable of enormous springs. The elk was more likely to be near deeply broken terrain and forest, even though it spent much of the year as a plains animal. Trapped elk were hard to hold unless the fence was high and strong.

Forest Indians were good at waiting for animals to come to them. They carefully studied waterholes and mineral licks frequented by deer or moose, then waited in a downwind blind to observe a cross section of the forest's population and choose an opportunity for attack at close range. Careful planning and camou-

Indians stalked deer by wearing
deerskin as camouflage, sometimes were able to
move into the midst of herds
and deliver arrows or spears at close range.
Animal skins were sometimes
used as moving decoys which could draw bands
of game into range of bows,
or entice quarry to stockades or natural
enclosures for capture.

flage almost always got them their game.

It was in trailing that the primitive Indian excelled anything the white man was able to do. The red tracker was a valuable member of white expeditions as long as unexplored country remained. He followed game through a study of subtle signs where no foot imprint was to be found, a skill depending not so much upon exceptional vision as upon a lifetime of attention to details of the wild world. To this day some of his signs are unexplained, but they included the crushed blade of grass, disarranged leaves, the rubbed stone. Much of his trailing speed came from knowledge of the quarry's most likely choice of route, a course that became obvious to one who knew the tactics of the pursued, and long segments of meandering routes could be quickly bypassed when the hunter established the general direction and located points the game was likely to pass. So the hunter might move much faster than the hunted, even though his prey was capable of great speed. If the hunter's guess proved wrong as he made shortcuts over long, winding trails, he could return to the point where he left the track and work out the puzzle more deliberately. To the uninformed observer such logic became magic.

The Indians may have been the greatest distance runners of all time. They could run down hoofed game in open country, a feat that is difficult but not impossible for hardened athletes, especially if they work in relays. The swiftest of deer soon tire if pushed; their bursts of furious speed last for only short distances. In open country a deer will be only mildly afraid of a man and might never get out of sight if pursuit is steady. When the animal finally realizes its full danger, it already has used most of its energy and relentless runners can catch it, playing on the knowledge that game tends to circle within a familiar range.

Where cover was dense, the Indian killed much of his hoofed game in its beds, using a system of trailing that involved a series of loops and a knowledge of the game's habits. Deer habitually feed in early morning and bed during the middle of the day. After leaving a feeding area, they are likely to move some distance to suitable bedding grounds, then travel in a short hook that enables them to lie downwind from the trail they have left, and close enough to see pursuers and slip away when they are sighted.

Learning that a trail ran toward good bedding ground, an Indian would leave it and begin a circle designed to intercept it farther on, a process simplified if the route was along an established path. When he intersected the trail again at the end of a loop, he would begin another circle. If he crossed the logical line of travel without finding a trace of game, he could assume that it had bedded somewhere between where he was and his last intersection with the trail. It was then that the hunt became a careful stalk, with all movements made upwind if possible. He hoped to come upon the bedded game from downwind, with the animal facing upwind toward its backtrail. If cover was thick and his movements were careful enough, a short-range bow was sufficient. It was a work of patience and care. Several minutes spent planting a moccasined foot silently were a small investment after hours of tracking.

Game in open country could be difficult to stalk, but after long watching antelope might be caught in an arroyo where they could be approached to within a few feet. Little groups or single animals were easiest to approach. Hours in a dry creek bed in the path of a feeding herd might be productive. Pronghorns often grazed to within a short distance and then stood confused at the sight of a momentarily unrecognized enemy. The

pronghorn of the days of Indian hunters was susceptible to "flagging," bringing them close out of curiosity to an object waved over a bush or from the crest of a hill. The same ruse worked hundreds of years later, especially with little bands of younger animals.

There is much confusion about the bear in Indian times. It is often difficult to tell whether historical records are referring to the black bear, which was seldom dangerous, or to the grizzly, a very different creature that could be expected to attack man without provocation. Although there were undoubtedly strong concentrations of grizzlies in many mountainous areas, the plains country was almost completely cleared by the middle of the nineteenth century.

Some Indian tribes venerated the black bear, and hunters of the eastern woodlands were honored for entering bear caves with spears. In some cases the bears might have been in semihibernation and there was no great danger. In others the hunter faced one or more sets of ready fangs and claws. Because of the bear's rough resemblance to human form when it walked on its hind legs, Indians sometimes felt brotherhood for it, even though they killed it for meat and skin. Bear hunts often were preceded by apologies to the bear and its spirit, and followed by ceremonies of both celebration and veneration.

Above the prairies and the forests the eagle was the king of birds and to the Indian he was an object of admiration, carrying long claws and a beak that could wound or kill. To both eastern and western Indians the eagle claw was a valued ornament, along with that of the bear, and the eagle's feathers added prestige to headdress or weapon. But like other creatures the Indian respected, the eagle was an object of elaborate hunting at times.

The eagle was trapped in pits baited with carrion. There would be a latticework of branches above the pit to hold the bait, and the Indian waited beneath it to catch the eagle's legs when it alighted. The bird could then be killed with a stone. Similar pits worked for wolves, although the hunter did not hide in the trap in this instance. Instead, he arranged the cover so that the wolf broke through, became imprisoned in the pit, and was killed at the Indian's leisure. There were other pits with roofs strong enough to hold the quarry, but with gaps through which a concealed spearman could drive up into the game's underside.

Simple snares were deadly for small game. A combination of snare and deadfall killed larger creatures. A deer pushing its head through a slip noose hung along a forest trail thrashed violently trying to escape, thus tripping a heavy log attached to the other end of the rope. The log's fall jerked the victim aloft and hanged him. For smaller game, the noose might be fastened to a bent sapling that would be released when an animal was caught.

The Iroquois had a noose trap for foraging birds. The hunter carefully cut a hole in a sheet of bark, spread it on an open spot in the winter forest and put seeds in a shallow declivity beneath the opening. Around the hole he placed a hair noose, easily drawn tight when a hungry bird caught its head in it as it withdrew after reaching the bait beneath the bark. The edge of the hole in the bark was a more effective support for the noose than the rim of an earthen hole, which might crumble.

An ingenious trap was set for the mink that disappeared and reappeared along the forest stream, testing the air and looking for danger with bright-eyed caution. When he caught the scent of In-

Indian hunters often cooperated
in building giant traps for herds of animals
and in driving quarry to
funnel-shaped enclosure that ended in a run
where they could be speared.
Snares often were fastened to bent trees which
straightened as animal tugged.
Below: Indian art depicted animals in their
relationship to the hunter.

dian bait, he traced it to a fallen log with a weathered woodpecker's hole, made one last survey of his surroundings, and put his small head through the aperture. Sharpened sticks, cleverly thrust through the log from the outside at just the right angle, held him fast at the neck and his struggles only drove them deeper.

Indians hunted and snared the upland birds, some of which, like the ruffed grouse and quail, were attracted to their settlement clearings. Where grassland was seldom broken by shrubs or trees, the prairie chicken was plentiful. Its closest relative, the heath hen, lived on the edges of the eastern woods; it became extinct when the thickening forest and the busy plow took over its places of residence. Where scattered woodland and wild rosebushes overlapped western prairies, sharp-tailed grouse found a home that tolerated civilization. The sage hen, largest of American grouse, lived on the high plateaus near mountain country where its essential sage grew in a mixture of grasses. If buffalo overgrazed the prairie, the tenacious sage marched down from the slopes and took hold, as it would continue to do when domestic cattle became too numerous later on.

Not only did the prairie chicken, sharptail, and sage grouse feed the Indian camps, but their spring mating displays were patterns for Indian dances. At dawn and evening the birds gathered on their strutting grounds and the cocks established territories with booming and stamping to impress the calmly observant hens. The widespread tails and booming challenges were copied and magnified by circling red warriors around a thousand campfires.

A patient hunter might be unseen at the border of a strutting ground and a host of Indian youngsters looked for eggs in prairie and sage with their miniature bows at the ready. In woodland they probably took advantage of over-aggressive ruffed grouse, which resented intruders at their favorite booming logs and attempted fatal bluffs with bristling hackles. Other woodland grouse could be approached at close range and struck down by an arrow, or even a well-aimed stone.

Indians built artistic duck decoys that were effective long before there were long-range weapons. These included elaborately stuffed birds made from the skins of real waterfowl, carefully removed and filled with grass. There were decoys fashioned from reeds, some with artificial heads and others with real duck heads attached to them; some of the best examples of "tule decoys" came from a Nevada cave, evidently left by an aboriginal civilization.

Even with satisfactory decoys, the Indian hunter had to be carefully concealed to get close enough for a shot with his bow. In some instances he waited in chill water up to his shoulders, concealed by emergent vegetation. Indians waded underwater, breathing through hollow reeds, and worked their way in among the ducks until they could catch them by hand. Others floated gourds among the waterfowl; once the birds began to ignore the gourds, a hunter would drift in, his head in a hollowed gourd with appropriate peepholes. He, too, caught ducks by hand.

It is accepted that the Indian and Eskimo developed very good arrows and fairly good bows, although they were for the most part less efficient than the bows of Central Asian and European military bowmen. The bow's development varied greatly in differing game ranges. Killing bison took a much more powerful bow than one adequate for whitetail. Another factor seldom considered is that a tribe's archery might degenerate as firearms came on the scene, or as hunting gave way to farming. So the bows found in use when the white observers first studied them might have been inferior to those of a hundred or two hundred years before.

In range, it is unlikely that early American bows could compete with European models, but the flint arrowhead had unique properties of penetration, the shape of its flaking adding to its cutting qualities. The aboriginal bow could make no cast approaching the range of modern tackle. When Saxton T. Pope, modern hunting archer, tested a large number of early American bows he found none that would cast more than 210 yards, a modest distance by current standards. His research indicated the California Indians made the best of all the aboriginal arrows he examined; the Eskimos had some of the most powerful bows. The obsidian points, because of better cutting qualities combined with a conchoidal edge, showed twenty-five percent better penetration than steel points.

There seems little question that the Indian's arrows could pierce deep enough to kill any animal he might meet, if his aim were proper. Indian arrows certainly pierced Spanish armor and would have gone through that of the Norsemen as well. In fletching, the early American attached his feathers in several ways. Eskimos inserted them in slits, some Indians glued them to the shaft, some used stitching, and the crudest form had no fletching at all. The Indians used what bowmen call a "pinch draw," or "primary release," taking hold of the nocked arrow in a pinching hold, and did not employ the modern "three-finger draw."

Ash was the best-known bow wood among northern Indians. Osage orange was used farther south. The forest Indians, despite the close cover they often hunted, preferred fairly long bows. When horses came to the plains, short bows were used by mounted men and fired from horseback, usually at close range. Old paintings by frontier artists show buffalo run-

ners firing with their bows held vertically, horizontally, and most frequently at a slant. Evidently they were held any way that worked best for the given direction of fire.

Indian quivers generally were made of skin and carried aslant across the back, so that the feathered end of the arrows came easily to hand over the shoulder. Whatever the exaggerations concerning the Indian's accuracy or power, there is no doubt he could fire rapidly. The red bowman had more firepower than the white settler armed with muzzle-loading musket. He could shoot about as fast as the man with a single-shot breechloader, and was outdone in speed only when the repeater came into use.

Even with crude tackle, a hunter who had played and worked with it from childhood could develop superior accuracy and might have great skill in hitting moving targets. It is likely that the limitations of his equipment reduced long-range accuracy, and it is possible that many of the earliest stories of Indian prowess grew in the telling. Although it is impossible to separate truth from fiction in these stories, it is agreed the red man used the bow and arrow with telling effect. Blunt arrows were sometimes used against the smallest game, and the flaming arrow was a common weapon of Indians who wished to burn their enemies' lodges.

On horseback, the American Indian became an archer second to none, using a short, flat bow backed by animal sinew that ran lengthwise and was then secured by crosshatching. So many are the stories of the warrior riding with his horse between him and the enemy, and actually shooting under the pony's neck, that the most skeptical modern archer must believe them. The stories become more credible than ever when we learn of rawhide straps especially designed to help support a rider as he clung to the off side of a running horse.

The bow and arrow were so basic in early hunting that they became objects of superstition and ceremony. In some tribes there were taboos against women or children handling the tackle and against anyone stepping over a bow. Once it had been defiled, it was washed in sand and water. The bows and arrows were distinctive and bore the decorations and special features of the special tribes that used them. Poisoned arrows were little used in America, although sometimes a tribe resorted to rattlesnake venom. The procedure was to goad a snake into striking a fresh deer liver; when the envenomed meat had dried, arrowheads were embedded in it. There is no evidence that this added to the points' efficiency; its value was more superstitious than actual.

Mastery of the bow and arrow came both in hunting and in war. There was a code of bravery and recklessness among many Indian tribes, a spirit often demonstrated in the war party organized for no other reason than to bring fame and "coups" (deeds to boast about) to the warriors. Sometimes it was a deliberate challenge to battle by the victims of small raids. Even tribes united firmly against common enemies might stage small but fatal sorties against each other. Part of the game was to be certain that the objects of a brief attack should know just where revenge for it should be directed. Great chiefs and medicine men might speak peace to neighboring bands, but they spoke of coups and daring to their own braves, and some of this spirit carried over into hunting. Hunting was a necessity, but it was also a sport, and if the sport was dangerous, so much the better.

It is 1840. All day the mounted scouts have ridden the ridges and draws and the pattern of the slowly moving bison herd is almost established; by day it moves slowly and steadily, leaving a cropped swath miles wide. Each night reports of its movements are made and assessed in firelit camps.

The bands of following hunters have drawn closer together, like an army going to battle. Little distance separates the clusters of campfires. For the time being the young braves are closely restrained and until the buffalo run has been made there will be no raids on the horses of rival bands. Several tribes are represented and their leaders hold nightly councils with great ceremony, for they are committed to a single enterprise.

Although food is scarce in some of the tipis, there are regulations against individual hunting forays and village police wearing the insignia of their station will see that no single hunter or small party tries to cut off a straying calf or old bull. Such an attempt, if blundered, might begin a general stampede and make necessary a completely new approach to the herd. Already the hunting parties are in open country, a long way from the good deer cover, and it would be a hungry march if the buffalo should escape.

For the time being there is special discipline in the Indian camps. Even the youngsters, with their miniature bows and ever-present escorts of camp dogs, are subdued and do not move far from the tipis. The Indian women are ready with their skinning

*Realism of Indian duck decoys was
heightened by use of skin
or feathers from species being hunted. Reeds
formed body and made decoy
buoyant. Sharptails and other prairie grouse
strut during mating displays
and were imitated in warriors' costumes and
tribal dances. Bears have been
residents of far places—and intrigue artists.*

knives and packhorses, and their containers for the meat they hope to dry when the chase is over. They hope for months of dried meat and pemmican, for new tipis, and robes to be used in the coming winter. The young men are attentive to their buffalo horses, the fastest, best trained, and most valuable of all Indian riding stock, and there is special care for the short, stiff bows. The arrows are marked with each hunter's sign so that his kill will be recognized. A few hunters will use spears.

On the day of the hunt all is in readiness. The medicine men have given strength to the bows and the bowmen, and they have called for the buffalo to feed their people and provide new tipis for the winter that will soon be on them.

Dawn brings a clear day, with only the usual prairie breezes. The herd moves calmly in early morning, with clumps of feeding animals wading in grass so thick there is hardly any dust. (In time to come the draws and creek bottoms might be lined with cottonwoods, but for centuries prairie fires have protected the grass from the intrusions of foothill shrubs and trees.)

It is best to make the run early, for night will come soon enough. The camps are packed and moving behind the hunters, more compactly than usual, the fever of the chase already showing in the women's speed in getting under way. Many of the horses are not loaded. They are herded and driven along with those carrying the tipis and other equipment, some of them with travois formed of tipi poles. In a few hours there may be loads of meat for the extra ones.

The mounted hunters are in a ragged skirmish line. They have ridden quietly to within a few hundred yards of their prey, taking advantage of the wind and the low, grassy hills. It is not until some of the nearest buffalo mill uncertainly because of their hazy view of danger that the signal is given, a gesture from a leader near the center of the hunter's line.

The hunter is ready. He wears a breechcloth and moccasins. His arrows are in a quiver across his back and his bow has been taken from its cover. There are painted signs on his horse's neck and two eagle feathers are fast to the rein of the simple bridle. The horse has been restless all morning; at the signal it races with the others, seeing the dark crowd of bison ahead and going into the wind, the tall grass whipping its legs and muffling the drive of its unshod feet. The bison herd begins to surge uncertainly and a light haze of dust rises above it as scattered groups push together and begin concerted flight. But the swift ponies have had their advantage of surprise and are already into the herd. The charge has broken into a hundred separate chases. The veteran hunter assesses his position and the shaggy animals before him.

The dust is thick and the roar of the stampede rises. The archer passes an old bull in its stiff, head-slogging run and rides alongside a younger animal that turns from his charge. The bow is ready. At the moment when the big calf shoulders against another animal and while it is unable to swerve from the hunter, the first flint point goes home, angled forward from behind the ribs. The buffalo horse, trained to avoid horns, turns from the game and the rider fires two more arrows before racing on in pursuit of another victim. The faltering calf is passed by the rest of the herd and crumples in the slowly settling dust behind the run.

Shortly the wind clears the air. The hunter's women find the three arrows with their familiar markings and begin the tasks of skinning and butchering. It will be some time before the braves return, some of them leading their tired horses along the trail of

*Following pages: Indians
carried both bows and guns after white men
joined them in the field. Trade
weapons were generally crude and simple, and
though Indian life made maintenance
difficult, red hunters used beadwork and
leather to decorate hunting
and fighting equipment. Once guns were acquired,
Indians became dependent.*

dead and wounded bison. The main herd is miles away and scattered. At dusk the campfires blink on the prairies and the hard work goes on, but there is celebration for there will be meat for all.

The buffalo was a fundamental source of life on the Great Plains. No other animal has exerted a stronger influence on a human culture. From the buffalo the plains Indian could acquire nearly every item he needed for existence: meat for sustenance, skins for clothing and tents, wool for spinning and weaving, chips for burning, bladders for holding water, bones and horns for use in making tools and weapons. When the buffalo were scarce the Indian went hungry and was sometimes poorly equipped to undertake other forms of hunting. When the herds eventually were destroyed, the buffalo Indians were helpless.

It is estimated that the buffalo herds may have reached their peak at about 1600 and there may have been sixty million of them at that time, moving constantly over an enormous and constantly changing range in what seemed to be random migrations. The range was altered by the buffalo themselves, being cropped closely as the bison moved to new grass.

The modern plains buffalo of the last thousand years are much smaller and evidently more agile than the prehistoric giant, but even these later animals are impressive creatures, with some bulls standing six feet tall at the shoulder and weighing as much as 3,000 pounds.

There was a woods buffalo as well, its numbers never approaching those of the plains, but believed to live mainly in eastern forests. A mountain bison was reported near the Pacific and in the western mountains, but both of these bison became extinct before there could be any scientific study of them.

The main bison range was bounded on the north by timberland near Hudson's Bay and cut off on the south by the chaparral and desert near the Mexican border. There were bands of them reported over nearly all of the eastern third of the country and some were found as far south as Georgia and northern Florida. The eastern buffalo probably migrated there because Indian hunting pressure and natural changes scattered them from their native plains.

When Cabeza de Vaca and other Spaniards described the buffalo, they thought them a sort of plains cattle, and the English name of buffalo is said to come from the French *boeufs,* meaning oxen. The buffalo has poor eyesight. Before the Indians used horses, they ambushed buffalo by smearing themselves with mud and lying in wait in the deep-cut trails to water, driving in their arrows or spears at very close range. Buffalo could be approached upwind to fairly short distances, and when Indians attempted a "surround" on foot or horseback they might get within a quarter-mile of a band without concealment. Some of the buffalo "charges" evidently were the efforts of befuddled animals to join their attackers, thinking they were groups of bison, and the buffalo also had a tendency to cross the path of pursuers, a failing of much wild game that seems to feel its escape is being cut off.

But the buffalo is dangerous in an unpredictable way, and the wounded adult can be a grunting, whistling, bellowing assassin, dangerous to a hunter horsed or afoot. On occasion, herds of confused beasts derailed trains and capsized river boats, peril that made the buffalo hunt a sort of warfare for the red man. If buffalo running was less efficient than some other forms of hunting, it was the dangerous sort of thing that

48

Buffalo running, a colorful way
for Indians to secure meat, was undertaken
as community enterprise.
Bows and short-barreled guns were used;
arrows were driven in behind
animal's ribs as horse was run alongside.
Buffalo horse was most prized
of hunter's possessions and buffalo runs
called for prayer and ceremony.

made heroes of hard-riding Indian braves.

The bison is powerful and faster afoot than its appearance indicates. It has a strong sense of smell, but no means or sense of concealment since it usually lived where there was no place to hide. It has always been a herd animal, acting in a mass and often stampeded. The leaders of a herd might attempt to ford a river that was too swift, partly frozen, or with a boggy edge in which heavy animals would sink, and the following hundreds or thousands would go blindly to their destruction.

Buffalo wallowed where shallow mud patches occurred, probably to discourage insects and to comfort their hides in the annual shedding of hair. If mud was not available, they rolled in dusty spots, the same ones often being used by hundreds of animals. Thus the wallows became deep enough to form waterholes that saved human lives in later years and were used by the cattle herds after that. A hundred years after the wild buffalo's demise, the old wallows remain as prairie pot-holes and serve as gathering spots for nesting mallards. And among the old wallows were similar pits that once were the caves of ancient hunters.

The bison was not a game animal in the currently accepted sense, and even if no Indian had camped on its trail, no railroad worker had eaten its meat, and no wealthy sportsman had tallied a score of kills, it would have died out with the settlement of the country. It could not live with beef, wheat, and corn. The Spanish horse gone wild is more adapted to survival; the wild burro can live where the buffalo would starve.

Herd animals, such as buffalo and caribou, were most vulnerable to entrapment by driving, their instincts causing them to crowd together in fright. There were strategically located cliffs and arroyos where animals were killed in this way for hundreds of years; one of the best-known buffalo jumps is in the Sun River Valley of Montana, where the residue of slain animals has been estimated at 25,000 tons. Such a trap could be sprung every two or three months unless the prairie had been burned off too closely in making a drive.

For the buffalo drive the tribal groups united in a common plan. For several days they expertly guided the bison's travel with an occasional robe waved from a hill or a small, smoky fire, and at the chosen time they began to bend a section of the herd toward a natural trap several miles away. Turned from their preferred route, the buffalo became restless. Jostling and shoving, they united in closer formations and followed their accepted leaders, probably old cows.

The trap might be a wide valley that narrowed to a canyon and ended in a sheer drop. As the valley walls closed in, a few of the bison broke into a jarring trot, and then into a bobbing run, dust rising about the high, rocking humps. The retreat accelerated. Soon it would be a stampede. So far the red herdsmen had been seen occasionally on high ground, dark silhouettes and brief gleams from flint spears. Now they appeared in lines on the valley's walls, others emerging from lower hiding places behind boulders or brush, yelling, leaping, waving robes and weapons. Piles of vegetation or earthen heaps filled the gaps, appearing as so many more hunters to the near-sighted, panicky bison. They thundered onward in the wake of their berserk leaders, and fell to their death over the waiting precipice. The hunt ended in a bellowing horror of crushed and broken beasts below the leap. The dazed survivors were killed by spears or arrows, and the labors of butchering began. Much of the meat was wasted, either rotting before it could be processed, or so covered by shaggy bodies

it was never reached by the hunters' knives.

When the plains Indians acquired horses, more and more tribes turned to buffalo hunting as the mainstay of their existence. The horses carried the Indian closer in the buffalo's trail, but it was not always an advancement in his welfare, for when he specialized too much he neglected the older ways. The Indian was already reducing the bison when the white man began to intensify the slaughter.

Some tribes were altered drastically by the horse. The Comanche was first known as a foothill Indian, living precariously in the edges of the Rockies, unable to advance far into the plains for fear of better fighters. Comanches were stockier people than the early plains residents, most of whom were capable of much faster travel in open country. Then the muscular Comanche legs clasped horses and the tribe became great riders, among the world's best. They hunted buffalo in the open, made cruel war against red and white man alike, and were among the most feared of western Indians. Some early observers stated they became fat and lazy because of horses, but fat horsemen are unusual and most primitive riders tended to leanness.

The buffalo runner's use of the bow is well understood from early literature and sketches. Horseback Indians liked short guns for convenience. Most of them used smoothbores long after rifles were popular, and the barrels of the early trade guns were frequently cut down for convenience.

It has been reported that the buffalo runner could reload his smoothbore at the gallop, holding it by the barrel with one hand and managing his powder flask with the other hand and his teeth, jarring the barrel to force powder from the barrel into the flashpan. He carried round balls in his mouth and the saliva caused them to stick to the powder and to the fouling from earlier shots, and wedge lightly in the barrel. Guns used for such hunting were usually flintlock "trade guns," often known as fusils or fusees. By 1840, many Indians had such weapons.

Winter, often a time of short rations for primitive man, brought snow and ice as natural entrapments for carefully herded game. On western slopes the buffalo might take refuge from driven snow in the scattered timber above the edges of watercourses. Higher on the hillside, hunters stalked, dull shadows, like those of the ever-present wolves, fading and then darkening as the storm rose and ebbed. Then, with howls of triumph, they struck, stampeding the bison downhill where they floundered through great drifts and sank in boggy and unfrozen ground. The hunters followed more slowly with spears, knives, and arrows.

Another winter tactic was to drive buffalo onto ice. Few heavy animals can cross glare ice well and the buffalo either fell into helpless heaps or overloaded the ice and broke through, quickly becoming prey to the hunters.

Buffalo tribes of the Great Plains were more nomadic than most other Indians, following the herds by necessity, and they were travelers even before horses came from Spain to change them to what the whites spoke of as "horse Indians" or "buffalo Indians." Through much of the year these tribes were on the move, although they had more or less permanent camps in winter, protected from storms. From such headquarters they might make only short hunting forays while living largely on the dried and smoked meat from their operations in mild weather. In open winters they continued to hunt.

The colorful plains Indian,

Winter was hard on both
animals and red hunters. Snowdrifts
immobilized heavy animals,
making them easy targets. Hunters'
tactic was to drive them
from safe ground and—as here—
pursue on snowshoes. Artists
of 1800's showed bison (below) as
Indians' dangerous game.

Eskimo spearman holds quiet
vigil beside seal's blowhole in Arctic ice.
Toggle-harpoon head was released
from shaft after piercing quarry, and line
enabled hunter to play and
retrieve his kill. Living in a hostile land
with limited materials, the
Eskimo became an inventor and mechanic more
resourceful than the Indian.

decked in fur, feathers, beads, and rawhide, and mounted on a swift, painted horse, had only a brief moment of glory—that time after he acquired horses, before the buffalo dwindled, while he had goods to trade with the whites. It lasted less than a hundred years, from the late 1700's to about 1870, but during the brief supremacy of the buffalo runner Indians migrated to buffalo country from forests to the east and north, and from mountains to the south and west, leaving their old homes and former ways of life behind them. But when the bison vanished, so did the glory.

Dwelling in the north, near the edges of permanent ice, are the Eskimos. There have never been many of these people, probably no more than 100,000. They are for the most part a coastal race and their icy land cannot accommodate large populations, because—as with the Indians farther south—there must be hunting space between villages. The origins of the American Eskimos are vague. They are thought to be among the most recent American arrivals via the land bridge from Asia. Their culture nearly duplicates that of peoples in northern Europe and Asia.

The ice hunter has problems more complex than those of the woodland tracker, for his landscape can change in moments, as ice breaks into moving rafts or heaves into new valleys or hills. The landmarks of yesterday may be gone tomorrow. Insulation from the cold stands between life and death, and there is no substitute if the supply of meat fails.

Though the resources of their northland are limited, the Eskimo and the Aleut have not moved southward. Instead they have learned to construct more ingenious tools and weapons than their contemporaries in more moderate climes. Some of their old-est weapons have been little improved for their purpose, even by twentieth-century technology. For example, in one of the Eskimo's deadly schemes against the Arctic carnivores he used baleen, or whalebone. This grows inside the whale's mouth as a part of the sieve that collects food, and is in the form of resilient plates, tough and durable; it was a mainstay of Eskimo mechanics long before it appeared in the white woman's corsetry. The Eskimo sharpened a piece of baleen and coiled it like a watch spring, tying it to prevent uncoiling. Then he froze it, removed the binding, and inserted it in a piece of frozen meat to be gulped by wolf, fox, bear, or wolverine. Warmed, the coil straightened in the stomach of the animal to become a fatal spear that thrust from the inside. Willow springs were used in the same way.

Birds provided much of the Eskimo's food, especially the migratory fowl that nested in the Arctic barrens and cliffs, and he paid special attention to hunting methods for them. Early Eskimos used a bird spear with three or four bone points, which gave a spread in case aim at the small target was not quite true; it was deadly for befuddled ptarmigan croaking petulantly on the Arctic tundra and relying on the concealment of snow or scattered stones. A sitting or even a flying bird could be victim of the Eskimo bola, several bones attached to a common center by thongs and thrown so as to entangle game if not to kill it. Californian and South American Indians used a similar tool.

Much of the Eskimo's game—walrus, seal, whale, and polar bear—was killed in the water or at the edge of it, and recovery was always a delicate part of the chase. The Eskimo devised special weapons to meet the challenge, most importantly a spearhead, or "toggle harpoon," of ivory, so designed that it detached from the shaft after thrust or throw and was

Buoys attached to harpoon
kept pierced seal from sinking, as
Eskimo followed in kayak
to subdue and land his game with line.
Nanook, the polar bear, lives
on ice and in water more than on land,
and is dangerous foe for
inadequately armed Arctic travelers.

held by a line. The head, sometimes tipped with stone, then turned at an angle and worked deeper under tension as the prize was hauled to solid ice. The multipronged spear was used for fishing as well as bird hunting. To catch fish, an ivory decoy might be suspended beneath a hole in the ice; casual curiosity was enough to bring the fish within spearing distance. The weapon was the forerunner of the steel gig.

Once a really large creature was killed, floats were as important as the harpoon or spear. A wounded quarry was followed as it towed an inflated bladder or skin on a rawhide line. If a harpooned seal dived, the relentless lift of the float brought it back near the surface and a kayak, the Eskimo form of canoe, could follow closely, paddled by furred hunters, hardly distinguishable at a distance from the animals they pursued.

The skin kayak has proved its hunting worth on cold water, its operators almost sealed in it, a boat as efficient in its home as the birchbark canoe proved in more temperate climate. The umiak, a larger craft of walrus hide, is built as long as thirty feet and might carry twenty people. It is easily rowed and it moved long ago with sails of gut. Both boats endured through centuries, difficult to improve, even though framed only with driftwood or bone. Modern materials can speed construction but are little stronger for their weight.

The sea-going mammals, such as walrus, seal, and whale, are vulnerable to the spearman because they must surface for air, and the seal hunt can be a patient vigil by a blowhole in the ice with the polar bear as a hunting competitor. Afloat, the contest becomes more evenly matched. The whale is a deadly hazard to a skin boat and the great weight of a walrus can be dangerous, even if the game is bent on escape. Such con-

frontations required hunters of great courage.

Seals on ice were stalked from behind ice ridges, or by a timeless crawl in which the hunter imitated the seal in a humping, furred progress, preferably from downwind and with the sun at his back. As the game looked for danger the hunter rested; as the seal dozed he squirmed nearer. Once within range, he hurled his spear, the snaking line maintaining the connection even when the wounded animal sought escape in the sea. From a kayak the seal might be speared at the ice's edge. When a blowhole was located in thick ice, the Eskimo might place an indicator in it to move as the animal came up for air. Since seals move swiftly, the vigil was wasted if the harpoon was not ready.

The walrus was a dangerous game for primitive man, perhaps fifteen feet long and capable of overturning or crushing a kayak, whether in anger or in frantic escape. Its ivory tusks are used to gouge shellfish from the sea bottom, as much as a hundred yards down, and they are dangerous weapons as well. The adult walrus has little to fear from other animals, except the killer whale. Before that destroyer, the walrus panics, and herds have been known to smash through Eskimo villages when the orca appears. At times the walrus feeds on seals, animals more wedded to the sea. A walrus must spend part of its time on land, sometimes dozing in herds like mossy dark boulders along the shore, now and then giving forth grunts, groans, barks, and bellows, noisiest of the Arctic natives.

The most fabled of the Arctic's creatures is the great white bear, growing as large as the brown bear of Alaska. It was both game and adversary for early Eskimos, an animal of unpredictable moods— now a killer that does not turn from the arrow or spear, and now a fugitive that hurries miles across the snow for fear of one trace of man smell. Eskimos killed the polar bear with spears and arrows before they had guns, sometimes using the bear's curiosity to draw him near enough, perhaps mimicking seals to provoke a charge.

The polar bear is the newest member of the bear family. Its remains have been found no earlier than the late Pleistocene era. It is constructed somewhat differently from other bears, with a much longer neck that well adapts it for inspecting its surroundings while in the water. It swims freely miles from land or ice, using only its front paws for brisk locomotion. Most of its life is spent hunting seals, a series of careful stalks and sudden rushes. The bear, only slightly yellow against snow, crawls flat on its belly when a seal is sighted. The approach is so cautious that Eskimos say Nanook pushes a block of ice ahead of him to make his camouflage complete.

There is variation in the lives of the Eskimo hunters. Those who depend on the caribou have followed the herds on the tundra as the plains Indians followed the buffalo, a few of them still living much as they did before the white man captured the buffalo Indians for the reservations. The caribou, still numerous in the North, is a close relative of the domesticated reindeer, a herd animal with instincts for predictable migrations. The herds are attended by Eskimos with caribou-skin tents. Eskimos living primarily from sea hunting build permanent villages on the shore, sometimes using sod or tundra in their construction. The snow house could be a permanent winter home, but more often is a quickly built shelter for transient hunters. The Eskimo adapted differently from the other red men. He remained in the ice and snow, he built goggles to ward off blindness, and he gathered driftwood rather than go into the forest. The animals he hunted adapted, too, but some of them, like the musk ox, were dull witted and easily approached.

The musk ox is a remnant, like the buffalo, unequipped to cope with a changed world. It is a strange creature that left its fossils in the central United States when the ice came down, but followed the melting glaciers north. In danger, the musk-ox herd moves into a battle formation the same as that adopted for centuries by the world's human infantry. Younger and weaker animals cluster in the center of a circle of furious bulls and mature cows that stand shoulder to shoulder in rising rage, the bossed heads lowered and each animal performing its rituals of battle. A musky scent is released from glands, the feet are restlessly planted, and the ground or snow is tested.

It is only the very hungry wolf that comes now. At other times he waits for the sick or the young straggler, and when he now advances a little from his circling party he meets a charging bull with sloping horns and quick, disemboweling points above hooves that thrust and trample. If the wolf retreats, or is killed, the bull moves back to his place in the battle line and the grim wait begins anew.

Although it survived the retreat of the ice and the centuries of primitive hunters whose bows and arrows and spears were efficient against it, the musk ox needed modern law to protect it from the modern rifle.

The red man changed America as he hunted, using fire to alter the woodland and changing the game ranges by his constant pressure on the herds, but his alterations were so subtle that they were accepted as due processes of nature by those who came later. Even the Indian or Eskimo did not recognize his own handiwork.

3. The

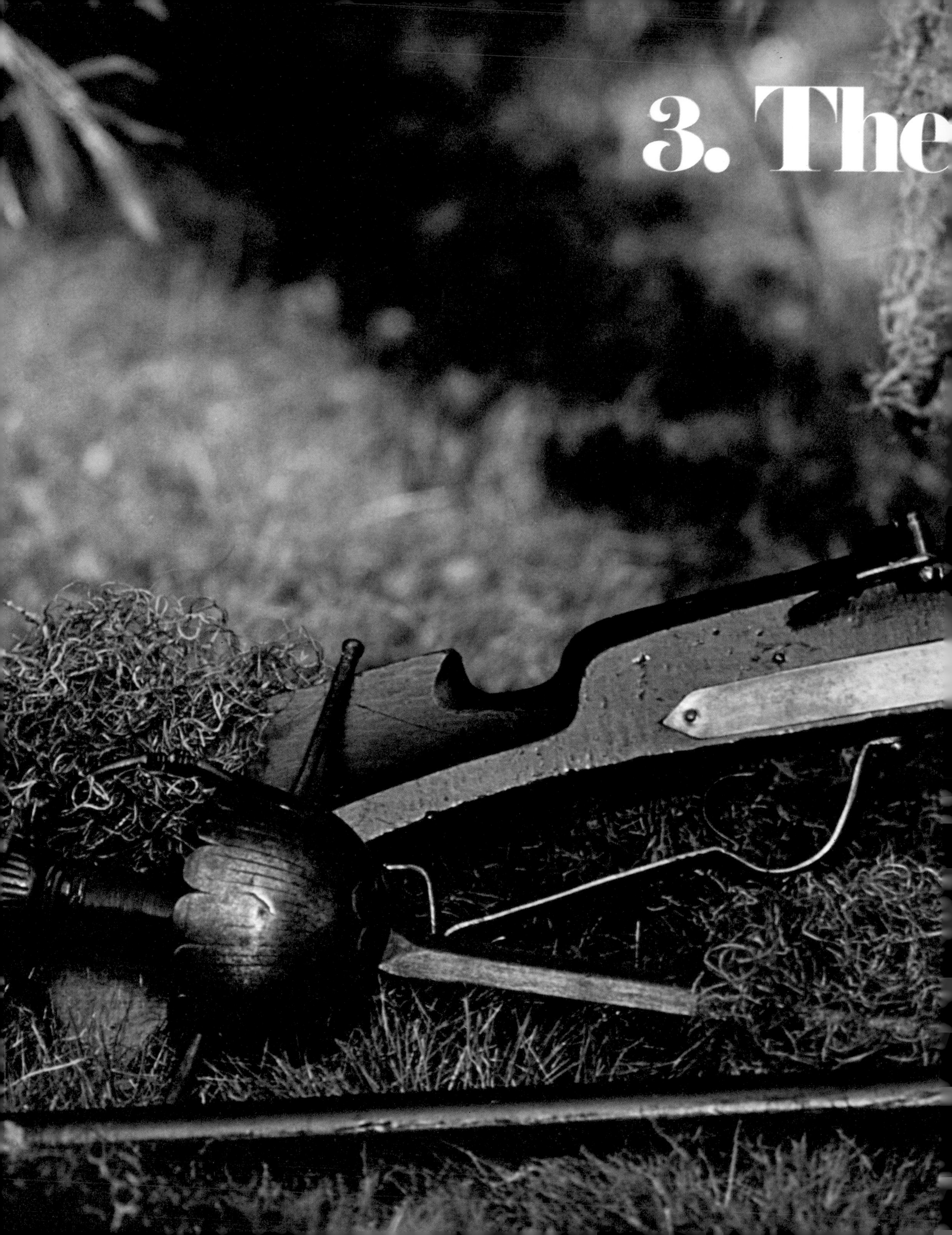

Explorers

Eventually, a white hunter in moccasins would tread America's Indian paths and game trails, a part of the land instead of its conqueror or victim. But he would be a product of the New World, developed through generations of frontier life.

Most of the first European explorers were soldiers and sailors, clumsy woodsmen who hunted only incidentally, by necessity. Of the newcomers, probably the Vikings were most like the native hunters. These warlike Norsemen sailed the Labrador coast and settled on the Newfoundland shores in the eleventh century. According to the sagas of their adventures, they found little difference between the caribou of the New World and the reindeer of their cold native lands. It was almost a thousand years ago that they disappeared from America, and it was only recently that their presence was proved and located in the ruins of their abandoned houses, confirming the truth of their sagas.

Extending the range of earlier voyages by wooden ships through Arctic mists, Leif Ericson had indeed brought his people to Newfoundland, where Norse arrows and spears had gathered the seal, whale, and tall-antlered deer. Leif's stay was brief but other Norsemen, setting out from Greenland, followed and established settlements. In Vinland (later proved to be Newfoundland), the Norsemen fought the American "Skraelings," who may have been Eskimos or Indians, or both, for Newfoundland was near the southern boundary of the Eskimo's domain. The Skraelings (a name that died, but was as appropriate as "Indian" or "Eskimo") used their skin boats against the invaders and matched their stone arrow points against the crude iron weapons and armor of the bearded enemy. Those "black, ugly men with shaggy hair on their heads," as the sagas described the Skraelings, may have marveled at the Norse arms and wooden ships, but they did not imitate them. No part of the Norsemen's more advanced war and hunting culture persisted in North America.

Although Labrador and Newfoundland, with their wooded hills and grassy caribou barrens, may have seemed familiar to the Norsemen, conditions were different for those Europeans who sailed the American coasts five hundred years later and landed much farther south. They had no plans for living off the game of a new land and they were in any case ill-equipped to do so. Most of them contemplated trading with the natives or enslaving them.

The eastern edge of subtropical North America was inviting, even if the inland forests were forbidding. The Spanish ships of the fifteenth and sixteenth centuries found a harbor along Florida's sandy beaches, and the inlets were easily navigated if the tide was right. Seaward sands protected inland lagoons fringed with coastal trees. The sands were then well secured by plants; later, due to man's meddling, they would shift continually. Anchored in the inland waters, where banks of oysters showed at low tide, the ships swung peacefully, but the wilderness inland rang with fearful sounds and hints of danger. At dawn or dusk, the vibrating roars of bull alligators filled the brackish marsh, more fearsome because they were not recognized.

The manatees' cow-like heads could have appeared as those of sea serpents across the inland bays, although the real dangers were water moccasins along the marsh borders and diamondback rattlesnakes in the sandy palmetto shade. Banks of marsh mosquitoes shifted with the winds, and the explorers soon learned the violence of tropical hurricanes.

The explorers of the new continent were ill-prepared for the western wilds or the virgin

Opening pages: Matchlocks
were first guns to reach American game fields,
and were intended as much for war
as for hunting. In Florida, Spaniards used
swords and pikes more often
than their awkward guns, which were slow and
inaccurate. But slow-moving game,
such as the opossum or alligator, was an easy
mark, and Indians were impressed.

timberlands of the East. They had hunted in a Europe that was, in the main, closely populated. Game there was conserved through necessity, and hunting was largely a prerogative of royalty—an amusement that usually required an army of attendants with emphasis upon the death of as much game as possible. Since the seventh century, when the Frankish King Dagobert had laid down regulations regarding the hunting of game, there had been game laws, most of them intended to preserve sport for the nobility. Hounds had been used in antiquity and falconry was popular with the European ruling classes, but America's forests were a new experience. Few of the first arrivals were versed in woodcraft or wilderness hunting, or even in the formal chase (although there were greyhounds with some of the Spanish expeditions, sometimes feared by the Indians and used as protection by their owners as well as for hunting). They knew how to trap rabbits, and this they did out of necessity. The Spanish were able to catch manatees and turtles for food, being well versed in living from the sea, and they learned some of the Indian's hunting methods. They found Indians roasting alligator whole and they may have learned to eat alligator tail. They reported killing crocodiles, but they may have confused their prey with the more plentiful alligators.

In truth, the Spanish and French explorers were better equipped for hunting men than game, armed as they were with swords, lances, and crossbows. For standing game, the crossbow was fairly accurate and quite powerful, although it was slow to reload, its stiff draw being set with a windlass. It fired a short bolt or arrow and had been well developed since the twelfth century, although early forms dated from more than a thousand years before. Those first explorers also brought guns to America. Soon these clumsy, muz-

zle-loading matchlock arquebuses would become readily portable hunting weapons, but for the time being they were inferior to the bow and arrow. They had been developed for warfare, and their inaccurate smoothbore missiles were better against massed troops than against a nervous whitetail deer. But there was some southern game they could fell: the opossum, for instance, that remnant of an early carnivorous age, which somehow survived despite its sloth-like habits. Its only defenses were a death-like unconsciousness when attacked, gleaming needle teeth that could wound but were most often bared only in a threatening grimace, and the ability to climb hand-over-hand to a high, swaying branch. In a tree it was an easy mark, and its carcass could feed two or three hungry Spaniards.

The black bear, difficult to approach on the ground, might take to a tree before the clank and clatter of a Spanish expedition—and there were black bears over nearly all America. The bear, a bulky, furry ball in a tree fork, may have thought itself safe, but it was vulnerable to the arquebus.

The matchlock, the beginning of modern firearms, was carried by many explorers. It was fired by a smoldering cord of slow-burning tow fastened in a serpentine and moved with a simple trigger. When the shooter had poured powder in the muzzle, seated a ball or several balls atop it, and primed the pan with powder, he could aim as best he could with crude sights (or none at all), and pull the trigger while an aide held the forked barrel support that had been firmly seated in the ground.

It was not a big-game gun, but if a breastplated Frenchman or Spaniard used reasonable caution and loaded his matchlock with a handful of shot, or even pebbles, he might do well in the sawgrass-bor-

The alligator, relic of another age, was a frightening thing to early explorers. They depicted Indians killing the reptiles with aid of long poles. But the alligator lived in such inaccessible places that it prospered until ravaged by hide hunters in twentieth century. New laws have since provided protection.

4

*Spanish explorers made captives and
beasts of burden of Indians
in a bloody series of American adventures.
Their armor was sometimes
pierced by Indian arrows, but their
arms were superior. Slavery
lasted for period of Spanish occupation.
Spaniards learned hunting
methods from their Indian victims.*

dered marshes, where he could fire into a close-ordered flock of bluebills, pintails, teal, or mottled Florida ducks. And if another hunter could cause disturbance from the flock's other side, the alarmed waterfowl might bunch even closer, long enough for the coarse black powder to do its work.

The matchlock was to become a lighter and more easily carried weapon. Before its development, a gun was fired by lighting a touchhole, but the matchlock, with all of its disadvantages, enabled the shooter to look at his target instead of at his match. It followed naturally that shooters would aim along the barrel and use sights, so the matchlock became a shoulder weapon and began to take the form of hunting guns to come.

About the time of Columbus, European inventors had begun to develop the wheel lock, a complex and expensive mechanism never to become popular on the frontiers, although some wheel locks reached America. The wheel lock included a rough steel wheel that was spun when the trigger was pulled. A dog-head vise holding iron pyrites pressed against it to cause sparks, somewhat like the contemporary cigarette lighter. At the same time, a cover was automatically moved away from the powder pan. The top of the wheel actually protruded into the pan's bottom. The mechanism had to be wound by a wrench, or spanner, before each shot.

Although the wheel lock was invented shortly after 1500, it was a long while before it was widely accepted, and then mainly as an arm for the rich. Some wheel locks were ornate showpieces. The guns did not lend themselves to heavy use. Only a few of the early white Americans used them. Besides their prohibitive cost, they were also delicate; such a mechanism had little place on the frontier, where only elementary black-

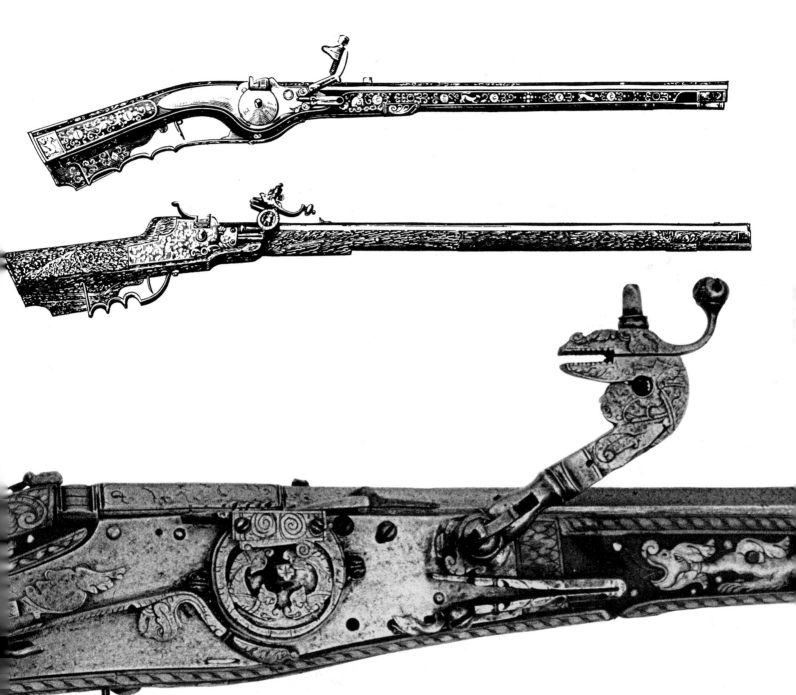

Spanish explorers such as de Vaca were
first white hunters in American
West. Intricate wheel locks, like three here,
were advanced but expensive
designs carried by wealthy colonists.
Simple and rugged matchlock was
basic weapon until coming of snaphaunce.

68

*Beaver were incentive for many
hunting expeditions into wilderness areas.
Unusual print (right) shows
beaver being killed in volley of gunfire. Man on
snowshoes is artist's impression
of frontiersman. Remington painting is portrait
of typical horse-packing
mountain man who followed westward trail
of French-Canadian voyageurs.*

smithing was available. It was the simpler matchlock and later the snaphaunce that most of the first settlers carried, although the wheel lock appeared occasionally during the transition.

Although much of Spanish exploration was a bloody conquest of Indian civilizations in the search for gold and silver, the Spaniards established many settlements. Their accounts of operations in the South and Southwest make frequent mention of the buffalo as a source of meat and hides, but there was little incentive for a fur trade such as later established by the French. When a great lode was discovered in Mexico in 1548, it was silver, not furs and buffalo hides, that went back to Europe on Spanish ships.

Many Indians were killed or enslaved, but there were many who cooperated with the Spaniards. It is oversimplification to state that the conquerors were never constructive in their Indian relationships. Indians hunted for the Spanish and exchanged skills with them. The Spanish expeditions that laid out the many *caminos reales* were forced to live from the land they traveled. There were dozens of Spanish trails in the South and Southwest; some were replaced by well-traveled roads and eventually by highways. Most of the trails were traced only by axe blazes on trees and by natural landmarks.

Spaniards sometimes lanced buffalo, or "Indian cattle," perhaps combining sport with meat hunting. The Spanish were met by French fur traders when La Salle came down the Mississippi to plant his flag at the river's mouth in 1682.

Both Spanish and French dried buffalo and porpoise meat and employed meat cellars. The French learned how to shoot buffalo at close range, aiming for the spine after discovering that this was the

Copyright 1890 by
Frederic Remington

*Voyageurs scouted new land
and water in their pioneering ventures. They
traded with Midwest Indians wherever
their canoes took them, and became a part of
Indian civilization. Opossum,
a relic of prehistory, survives with more
intelligent animals despite man's
hunting, trapping, and settlement. Moose has
required protection for survival.*

*French hunters and traders
made friends with Indians and adopted their
ways in the wilderness. Birch
canoe was a masterpiece of Indian work,
serving as shelter and as
conveyance in Northeast expanse knitted by
lakes and rivers. Although
whites had better tools and knew shipbuilding,
they could not improve it.*

most effective spot for felling the big animals with low-velocity, under-powered guns.

The most revolutionary change in the Indians' life was brought about by the horse. Indians acquired some horses through trade with the Spaniards, stole others, and took advantage of the inevitable strays that were lost by the numerous expeditions. In a surprisingly short time, many tribes acquired fine herds and transformed themselves into "horse cultures."

In the North, the French woodsman-trapper appeared, one of the first of the breed which was to crisscross the continent on a thousand game trails, breaking the way for civilization and either fading before it or being absorbed by it.

The French-Canadian hunter, trapper, and trader accepted the Indian and the Indian's way of life, and fur trading was the object of the first footholds of the French in the St. Lawrence River area. From Quebec and Montreal the French joined the resident Indians to spread across a northland where cold winters made the beaver's fur thick, and swift rivers were highways for bark canoes.

The French-Canadian voyageur was a product of the fur trade, a backwoods freighter and hunter with skills handed from father to son in a proud, rough and independent existence. He accepted the Indian's canoe and adapted it. There were bark canoes thirty or forty feet long, with crews of as many as fourteen paddlers, carrying tons of trade goods on the larger rivers. They were unloaded at night and became dry-ground shelter for the crew. The voyageurs sang as they swung their paddles, and where the rivers finally became small streams they met smaller canoes paddled by Indian, French, or half-breed woodsmen, who exchanged bales of beaver, marten, and mink for the voyageurs' trade goods. These men worked the finer threads of the fur-gathering network. They turned their canoes back to the depths of their lonely land, and when the song of the departing voyageurs was lost in the distance, there was only the gurgle of the current and the gentle thrust of the paddle to be heard. They would reconnoitre beaver dams on the smaller brooks and make a moccasined search for mink tracks in the silt at the stream's edge. The trapper's busy eye would catch a ribbon trail of mud coming down from the working beaver pond on a tiny tributary, and he looked for fresh cuttings, and most of all for the fresh drag trails marking the beavers' haul of provender toward a winter's lodge. The trapper automatically watched for a place where abruptly deep water would make a trap setting practical and looked for moose tracks along the marshy areas. He needed not only fur but meat. The wolverine's track was unwelcome, for a trapper might carry on a losing contest as the "Indian devil" stole his catch.

The wolverine, a bear-like marauder of the Canadian wilderness, is one of few wild animals believed to destroy maliciously. A gluttonous eater of anything available in the form of meat, it could learn to follow a trapline, and many a trapper has been forced to change his operations when he found the "devil" was moving ahead of him on his rounds. The wolverine, weighing only thirty-five to sixty pounds, is a terrible fighter and feared by many larger animals. It has shown an uncanny ability to avoid traps. Dark brown, short-legged, and bushy-tailed, its very appearance suggested evil to the minds of explorers who met it.

The canoes went farther and farther as years went on, and the trappers shook their heads and said the beaver would some day be trapped out. The voyageurs and French trap-

74 *The wilderness beaver dam*
alters valleys, can produce lakes that will
later change to swamp and
then to grassy meadows. French traders
followed watercourses to
beaver country, staying in the wilds for long
periods and returning to their
settlements with heavily laden canoes. The
St. Lawrence was a main route.

Ruffed grouse is emblem of the wild America that awaited the first explorers. Although it could live at edge of the farm, it never became tame like many other birds that began as wild game and were domesticated. But it was sometimes an easy mark for travelers on the frontier.

pers had their day, beginning with Samuel de Champlain's first voyage to Canada in 1603 and overlapping the brief time of the Rocky Mountain man in the early nineteenth century. They wore deerskin or moosehide moccasins and deerskin trousers, to which they added a knitted cap and a brilliant sash. They drank and fought during their brief visits to Canada's trading posts and boasted of their speed with the paddle or their strength with the tumpline. A headband attached to the pack harness, the tumpline distributed weight and enabled a man to carry incredible loads for short distances on rocky portages. The isometric tension developed the voyageur's neck to wrestler's proportions.

Through long use the deerskin clothing acquired a greasy patina and the wearer's beard and hair would be unkempt from months of exposure and untold nights of campfire smoke. They were rough men, those who brought or sent the thousands of beaver plews to Montreal so that dandies in the eastern United States and the capitals of Europe could sport their choice beaver hats.

The Canadian trappers and traders were products of the raw, new land, with only fragile ties to their mother countries. They were entrepreneurs of a sort, content with riches on a far lesser scale than those sought by the high-born explorers who came in search of gold and glory for their flags. France and England might be at war for the wilderness, but the French and English mingled with common cause at fur-trading centers in Montreal, then at Quebec and Hudson's Bay. These North American hunters were developing their own patterns and their own ways of life.

European hunters who ventured north of the St. Lawrence found the Indians killing "elks," perhaps a misnomer for the American moose which is virtually a duplicate of the European elk. In the late sixteen-hundreds, the Indians of eastern Canada and their white guests made camp where big game fell, building temporary bark tents and consuming the meat before moving on. There was snowshoe hunting in winter, with moose driven from their wintering yards and into crusted drifts where shooting was easy. On Lake Champlain, Indians built blinds and used decoys for ducks and geese, either shooting the game or using nets like the nineteenth-century wildfowler. These decoys were stuffed bird skins fastened to small planks to keep them afloat.

Canadian hunters of the seventeen-hundreds encountered the passenger pigeons, often so thick that they became a nuisance. At one time the pigeons were "excommunicated" by the Bishop of Montreal. Their larger part in American hunting would come more than a hundred years later.

Game, as well as its habitat, would change in later years. The ruffed grouse of the Northeast, difficult prey for a later hunter, was a "wood hen" that sat in trees in flocks and could be killed one at a time by Indian arrows. During the spring mating season, the hunters followed their drumming sounds. (Perhaps the first American bird dogs were those that scented grouse in their trees and barked till the hunters came.)

Two hundred years later the New England grouse hunter looked for a brown-feathered missile, using carefully trained dogs and quick shotguns. The grouse seekers who went west by stages over many years found tame birds that had not yet learned to avoid man and his devices. In the twentieth century, the grouse of northwestern Canada was still a "wood hen" that sat in willows and conifers at borders of new clearings, staring stupidly at dog and hunter.

Other game was wild enough to be tame when the first explorers met it. The moose was a ready source of meat for the voyageurs and is still easy to approach in some of the wildest corners of Alaska and Canada. Wild ducks were much tamer than most of the twentieth-century birds, if today's unhunted waterfowl of remote sections are typical of the early game.

Early American wanderers used venison killed in Indian fire hunts and reported some circles of flame five miles in circumference. Laying such a fire required careful study and considerable personnel if the fire line was to contain the game, for the blaze must start around the entire area at about the same time. It was in connection with Indian contacts that explorers first mentioned efforts at game conservation. They reported that Indian hunters did not kill female deer—at least in part of their mass entrapments—the choice being simple for archers or spearmen once the game was enclosed.

As settlers became firmly established in the seventeenth century, they began the first changes of game cover. Before long they acquired the best European hunting weapons and modified them to suit their purposes. European ideas about hunting were largely forgotten.

4. First

Settlers

preading over a large area of the forest floor, the band of turkeys moves constantly, communicating now and then with subdued murmurs. A young bird finds he has strayed temporarily and yelps stridently until there is an answer from another member of the flock. There are intermittent rustlings as the birds scratch for acorns in the carpet of duff, or make brief pursuit of an insect that has survived the early autumn frosts. Although most of the flock is looking for food there are always one or two heads held high and watchful, inspecting the surroundings for possible danger.

The flock is part of the plentiful turkey population that inhabits the Massachusetts forest in 1650. The crudely armed hunter who stalks them has learned that although they are numerous, they are not to be had without considerable woodcraft.

The oak forest is mature and fairly open, although there are brushy streaks along the brooks, some of it blackberry and sumac. Sun comes through the trees in blotches, but it is already late enough for most of the ground to be in shadow; the large, bronze birds are beginning to merge into the gloaming.

Feeding becomes more brisk as evening comes on. During the midday hours it was desultory and the flock seemed to wander aimlessly, while in small forest openings some of them had dusted so vigorously that the streaks of sunlight appeared smoky. In late afternoon the flock regrouped loosely, with a minimum of calling. Traveling slowly, the birds left dark areas on the ground where their scratching overturned and exposed the damp undersides of fallen leaves.

It had been a clear morning and the turkeys had moved restlessly on their perches with the first light, their necks twisting and turning as forest sounds increased. When they were able to see the ground plainly they dropped down, with much flapping, and bunched noisily, yelping at each other. If it had been foggy or rainy they would have stayed on the roost until midmorning, but in the clear fall weather they began their day early. Crows flew over the treetops, cawing to each other as they left their own roosts and made occasional swooping glides to inspect the forest floor below.

Once, as the troop skirted a grassy opening, they met a whitetail buck on the way to his daytime bed; they stopped momentarily as he passed. Gray squirrels were busy in the oaks overhead. Several of them left the ground to make way for the turkey advance and then barked petulantly from low perches.

During the early morning the flock was approached by a bobcat, but it gave him a wide berth and clucked a curt warning of his presence. The cat, crouching slightly and almost invisible against a low bush, studied individual birds, but there was no sign of weak or unhealthy prey and he disappeared to search for other food. He was never close enough for a charge. As he left, a squirrel rattled disapproval from a beech.

In midafternoon the hunter left his cabin in a clearing and quickly entered the open forest. It has been twenty years since white men first hacked out fields and planted natural openings in this part of New England, and already some of the small plots are being abandoned because constant farming has worn the soil and shrunk the yield. Where the forest stood there are now plots of broom sedge, and some of the edges are growing to blackberry and greenbriar as the wood slowly begins closing in again. It is a process that has continued for centuries and there will be new clearing again to complete the cycle.

The hunter is a farmer rather than a woodsman, and although he harvests from the

*Opening pages: America's own
rifle was the Kentucky, descendant of German
jaeger, but with longer barrel
and special requirements for frontier use
in simplicity of mechanism. Highly
accurate when compared to smoothbore guns, the
Kentucky went westward
with explorers. Its bore was satisfactory for
whitetail, black bear, and squirrels.*

forest, he sees it as an obstacle to his progress, an adversary to be defeated by backbreaking labor with axe and saw, a harbor for wolves that may raid his sheep. As he enters the forest, climbing over a fence that is part stone and part logs, he starts instinctively from the roar of a ruffed grouse that leaves a clump of bushes and is gone somewhere deep into the tree shadows. He has set snares for grouse, but he is less successful than his Indian neighbors and is learning that the grouse prefer the borders of his cleared land to the heavy timber. He has even killed grouse with a stick occasionally, but he never considers using his crude gun on a bird in flight.

In the forest he stops at frequent intervals to look and listen for the game and to locate familiar landmarks. He may return home after dark and it will be difficult unless the direction is carefully noted. He has traveled less than a mile when he finds marks signifying that the turkeys have scratched only a little while before. They have moved along the bends of a stream; he walks faster, trying to make as little sound as possible, and making a wide circle, hoping to meet the band farther along. When he turns back to the stream he sees no fresh signs of scratching, and he sits down in the leaves behind a windfallen oak whose trunk is large enough to make a rest for his matchlock. Now he devotes his attention to the route he believes the turkeys will take. It is one of the suspicious squirrels that gives him away, squalling and barking, its tail jerking in emphasis from a perch ten feet up.

The feeding turkeys stop and stare unmoving for a few moments and then individuals move slightly and cautiously to the nearest concealment, their necks stretched for the best view. Although the hunter stares into the forest with special attention to the brushy areas, he can see nothing to aim at. Once he sees a pair of long, slender legs but the body is blocked from view. He stands up and walks briskly toward what must be the flock's center. His hunting plan has changed. Now he sees birds running in nearly all directions and several fly off through the woods, but there is no chance for a shot, even when one flushes almost at his feet, a twenty-pound bird that has somehow remained invisible in the skimpy concealment of a fallen branch of oak. His gun is heavy and slow and he has never fired at a moving target.

In a few moments there is no sign of the flock. Most of the birds have run at high speed for fifty yards or so and then slowed to a fast walk with frequent changes of direction. Several have flown for a considerable distance, but the hunter makes no effort to follow. He conceals himself behind another windfall and settles for a long wait, knowing a scattered flock is likely to reassemble where it was first frightened, and believing it will roost nearby.

Little more than an hour later it begins to gather in the general area from which it scattered. The breeze dies almost completely as night comes on and the hunter can hear distant yelps, but the sun is gone before he actually locates the roost on the shore of the stream. He moves toward the spot and hears other birds leaving the ground in another direction, so he knows he is near the center of the roost, for wild turkeys do not crowd their resting trees and the hunter will find no more than three or four together. His light is gone and he turns back toward his cabin. It is a difficult walk at night, but finally he sights the yellow square of his window. The hunt is not over, for he will be back in the woods long before dawn.

For the first part of his next morning's journey he carries a lantern for guidance, the

*Wild turkeys were a staple
of the earliest white residents and lived in
clearings and open forests close
to settlements where they were killed on
their roosts by the farmer's
matchlock. Sport and necessity were
combined in early hunts and
the small clearings were attractive to many
game species because of new growth.*

enormous shadows of his legs grotesque in the undergrowth. If a deer had stood fascinated by his light he might have chosen it as a target instead of a turkey, but no deer appears and he continues toward the turkey roost before he puts out his light and stands for some minutes adjusting his eyes to the night.

Once he hears the faraway howl of hunting wolves, but the thread of sound is soon lost through a vagary of wind. There are owl calls and an unidentified animal rushes noisily away, its progress becoming suddenly quiet as it begins to creep instead of flee. As he nears the stream where the turkeys are roosting he feels carefully for each step. A light frost has outlined some of the grass and shrubs, barely picked up by starlight, and with his lantern extinguished he is conscious of the smoldering tip of his gun's match. He is careful not to look directly at it and ruin his night vision.

On one cautious stop there is a different feel to the grass and ground and he knows he has reached a marshy spot next to the brook. Standing quietly, he hears a light gurgle where the stream crosses a log. He retreats a little way and looks up into indistinct branches that break the pattern of the stars. It is just a little lighter to the east; the glow increases as he makes a special effort to pick out roosting turkeys.

He is confident of his location when he hears a movement overhead, a bird that has either awakened with the growing dawn or has heard his cautious progress below. When he finally sights his game it is two birds on a branch that extends over the stream, a position often chosen for roosting because of the protection it offers from ground predators. They are simply two dark blobs erasing sections of the fading stars and he gropes for a rest, finally feeling a sapling with a crotch at about shoulder height. The match of his gun—a slow-burning cord locked in a serpentine—is a nuisance as he attempts to aim at the turkeys, for it partly blinds him as he stares along the uptilted barrel.

Now it rapidly grows light and he hears several turkeys stirring. The one he has chosen suddenly stands up on its limb, in silhouette. It is either preparing to drop to the ground or has been startled by the glowing match. He aims as best he can and pulls the trigger. The gun gives off a bright flash from the pan, an enormous flash from its barrel, and the hollow, thudding report of coarse black powder. Blinded by the flash, the hunter knows he has hit only by the dying flops of the big bird at the edge of the brook. He tries to reload quickly, but his fingers are cold. All about him the turkeys are leaving. He has no other chances, but it has been a lucky morning, worthy of some buckskin-clad professional who will appear a generation later.

The wild turkey has faded quickly wherever hunters have pursued it hard. Its habits are predictable, and the hungry frontiersman could learn its ways and be as deadly as the poachers of a later time. Where New England settlers cut back the forest, the turkey disappeared, although it served a purpose in feeding the first farmers. In other parts of America it clung in reduced numbers and habitat. A turkey killed in Massachusetts in 1851 was believed to be the last of the original native stock.

Wild turkeys occupied much of the East and Middle West when Europeans arrived. Indians of the Southwest domesticated them, using their feathers ceremonially and their bones for tools. Some ancient arrows were tipped with turkey spurs. Certain tribes seemed to keep flocks without using them for food. The turkey was a mysterious part of the frontier, and those who described certain species as poor table fare may

The matchlock (top) was first
type of gun used by American hunters and was
followed by complicated and
expensive wheel lock (center) used by
European noblemen. The
snaphaunce lock on pistol (detail at right)
was predecessor of the flintlock
that was basis for the earliest Kentucky
rifles and Revolutionary muskets.

*American gunsmithing began
with small shops in Pennsylvania, where the
Kentucky rifle and its descendants
developed as improved models of Old World
weapons. Early arms were truly
custom equipment, made to meet whims of
frontiersmen who might be a
long journey away from gun repairs and who
needed arms for their livelihood.*

have confused the true turkey with the carrion-eating turkey vulture.

The domestic turkey, a boon to man, was a curse to the wild relatives from which it originally descended. It went to Europe with some of the earliest Spanish explorers and later returned to America, carrying domestic poultry diseases that defeated early attempts, made in the middle of the twentieth century, to rebuild the decimated wild ranks. There were years of hopeful introductions and interbreeding between wild and domestic birds before game managers began to appreciate the delicate balances and sense the frailty of the wild bird's ecology.

While colors are much the same, the tame bird simply cannot exist in the wild and generally degrades the wild birds with which it comes in contact. Those that have repopulated much of the original range, as well as spread to new country, have carried the long legs and quick wings of their early ancestors. Although there must have been some crosses between domestic and wild strains, the new residents have the characteristics of wild birds. By the late nineteen-sixties new crops of wild ones had returned to the forests, fed at the edges of superhighways, and even left their long-toed tracks in the newly turned earth of housing developments.

The wolf met the farmers at Jamestown as soon as livestock arrived there in 1609, and even in the days of the Revolution farmer-soldier morale suffered with word that wives at home were losing the war of wolves. The wolf, with every hand against it, was pushed out of the East, only to renew its fight in the Midwest and West. In 1717 colonists considered building a fence across Cape Cod to make a livestock sanctuary of the outer Cape, but those on the mainland side felt the wolf pressures would be increased for them. By 1800 the

wolves were almost gone from New England and eastern Canada. The last Maine wolf was killed in 1860, but a few remained in Pennsylvania and upper New York State until the twentieth century.

Hunters of the late eighteen-hundreds found that gray wolves traveled mainly in small family groups, although settlers of 1700 reported packs of hundreds. Perhaps the true wolf packs disbanded for survival; later studies concluded that the groupings of colonial times were short-term associations. If attacks on humans were rare, the killers were in no terror from a farmer who could deliver only a single, poorly aimed shot without laborious reloading. Although one of the first New World animals to be greatly reduced in numbers, the wolf came nearest to stopping the farmer's advance. In colonial days there were professional wolf hunters and some sport hunters. Hounds were often used to course wolves.

The eastern whitetail deer was plentiful during the eighteenth century, although it is doubtful that it reached the numbers of the nineteen-fifties. There were elk and moose in the Northeast, but since the American moose was virtually a duplicate of the animal the Europeans called elk, it is difficult to tell from old accounts how plentiful the wapiti was.

The cougar was a hazard to livestock and was killed at every opportunity. John Lawson reported in 1711 that it was the chief hazard of all the predators in Carolina. Although it was never the object of such organized destruction as that which followed the wolf, bounties were paid religiously. It was no longer an important eastern livestock predator by 1850. Of the large animals the cougar was most difficult to hunt.

Along the seaboard there was uncontrolled killing of sea turtles during colonial days

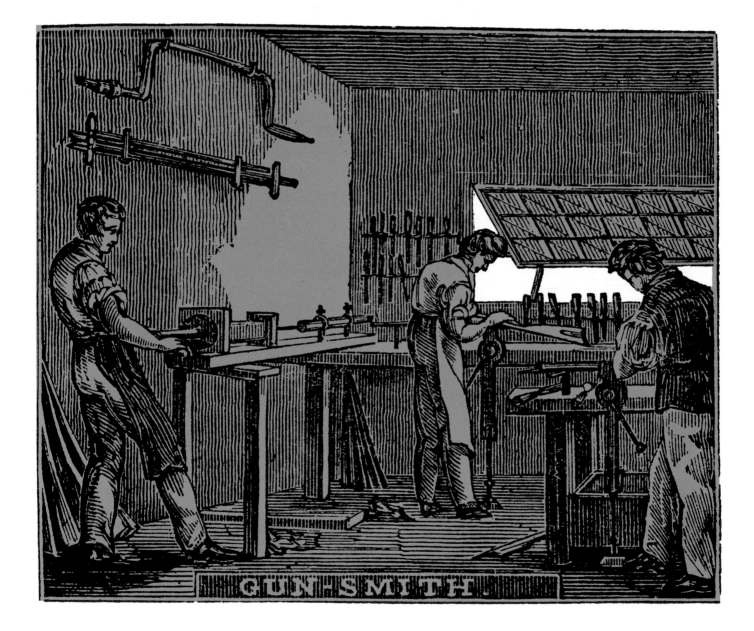

GUNSMITH

*Kentucky design was followed
by many variations. Over-under piece (far left)
carries ramrod on side.
Set triggers were common on long rifles.
Over-under is percussion; fowling
piece beside it is flintlock. Ornate gun
in inset is decorated German
jaeger, type of arm from which squirrel rifle
was designed in Pennsylvania.*

and they never recovered from it. Turtles were easily captured when they came ashore to lay their eggs, which were a delicacy.

Settlers had less impact on the Florida wildlife because swamp terrain made very difficult hunting compared to the open forests farther north. None of the larger animals was ever completely wiped out of its Florida habitats. Black bear, deer, bobcat, and alligators survived the period of uncontrolled hunting.

The passenger pigeon migrated, roosted, and nested in droves in northern forests. Never a gamebird—it could be killed by sticks or stones thrown into its massed airborne ranks—and unable to compete with birds of more individual cunning, yet it survived for a time by sheer force of numbers.

The great waterfowl flights came in spring and fall. The birds were easily collected by smoothbore ambushes, but most of the hunters who shot them knew neither where they came from nor where they went. The game supply seemed endless and for all time.

The accepted frontier line of 1774 split what is now Georgia, ran north through the western edges of North and South Carolina, and then bent westward through part of the Appalachians. In the North it extended as far west as Albany. Other routes of expansion came south from Canada and spread from Spanish settlements in the Southwest. Daniel Boone's exploration of Kentucky from North Carolina in 1769 opened new lands to the hunter and he then opened the Wilderness Road through Cumberland Gap to establish Boonesboro. Those who followed him were some of the first hunters to move still farther west.

The first settlers carried the matchlock, which was inferior in both speed and accuracy to the longbow. But even as the first clearings were being cut, Europeans were building the snaphaunce, which used flint to strike a spark and quickly ignite a charge of powder. The snaphaunce was the beginning of true efficiency in easily portable guns. Myles Standish was said to have carried one on board the *Mayflower*. Although it was a long while before most New World farmers could afford the snaphaunce, the short transition from it to the flintlock was quickly made. The flintlock featured an integrated mechanism: The cock, or hammer, drove away the cover of the powder pan as it descended to strike its flint against a battery or frizzen, and the flame thus produced ignited the charge inside the barrel through a flash hole.

The wheel lock was a relatively expensive and complicated mechanism used by rich Europeans. It saw service in the colonies as well, but was delicate for rough frontier use. The matchlock, wheel lock, snaphaunce, and flintlock musket came from Europe, as did the first rifling. Around 1750 a distinctly different form of American hunting gun had evolved from these European antecedents. In time it would be known as the Kentucky rifle, after the sharpshooting "hunters of Ken-

Following pages: Wild turkey
is among most wary of game birds, able to
escape by air or ground, and
has been brought back to comparative plenty
by careful management. Early
flocks were depleted by gun and farming
practices, but propagation-planting
has returned birds to the old habitat and
brought flocks to new ranges.

tucky" who distinguished themselves in the American wars. It developed together with America's own long-rifleman, and it derived from the needs he specified in blacksmith shops at the great forest's edge.

The Kentucky's immediate ancestor was the jaeger rifle from Central Europe, which used tight bullets that the shooter rammed into the rifling with the aid of a wrapping of greased cloth or leather patches. It was large-calibered and fairly short in the barrel. This gun, which took its name from the German for "hunter" or "gamekeeper," accompanied immigrants to Pennsylvania and served as a departure point for Pennsylvania gunsmiths in making a rifle that answered America's needs. They pared weight and made calibers smaller, so that the frontiersman—who traveled far on foot—would be as little encumbered as possible by the weight of his gun and bullets. To achieve greater accuracy in what was essentially a hunting gun, they lengthened the barrel for better sighting and more complete burning of the scarce black powder. And these unknown artisans bestowed on the new American rifle a graceful shape and full-length stock that pleased the rough and unschooled men who carried it as tool, weapon, and prized possession.

The Kentucky rifle had another advantage in its flintlock mechanism. Although the best flints came from Europe, it was always possible to find pieces of flint or agate in the wild to use as substitutes. When percussion guns began to be used, some rifles were converted to the new system but there were other frontiersmen who actually had percussion guns converted to flint, figuring it would be a worse situation to run out of caps than out of flints.

The black powder of the day was a combination of sulphur, saltpeter, and charcoal which varied in proportion of ingredients from lot to lot. Each frontier shooter studied the requirements of his own rifle, learned its most effective charges, and experimented with each purchase of powder.

The barrel of the Kentucky rifle was soft and tended to lose accuracy with heavy use. The gunsmith's method of renewing its efficiency was simply to enlarge the bore to take a heavier bullet. Thus, calibers were far from standard, and with its unique combinations of powder and bullet the rifle was as much an individual as its weatherbeaten owner.

The long gun on occasion has been called a squirrel rifle and, indeed, some of the lighter calibers were designed primarily for small game. Those of less than .40 caliber were not excessively destructive to squirrels and birds since velocity was low—seldom more than 1,700 feet per second (as against well over 2,000 feet for modern arms firing elongate bullets). Some users of the heavier calibers reputedly "barked" squirrels by striking a tree limb beneath the animal's head—a performance not beyond the gun's capability. In most cases the ball actually broke loose enough wood to stun the squirrel, it is said. Some "barkers" claimed the jar of the bullet's impact was sufficient to cause the animal to fall from a small limb. "Barking" is not difficult with modern high-velocity rifles. For the frontiersman it was a demonstration of skill but not much used in meat hunting.

In any event, the better Kentuckys had all the accuracy their owners required with the sights employed. The long barrel—more than forty inches in the finest rifles built shortly after the Revolution —gave great sighting radius and was naturally muzzle heavy for steady offhand holding.

The long rifle did not fit the European ideas of military weaponry. Even a woodsman

Marksmanship was matter of pride for early white families and shooting match was a social event of great importance, often with live turkeys as prizes, and sometimes as targets. Loads for the flintlock were an individual matter and lots of powder varied.

who lived with his rifle could not push the patched bullet home as quickly as a European infantryman could load his smoothbore musket. And the Kentucky was not for hand-to-hand fighting or for firing at massed troops. But as a sniper's rifle, fired from ambush at considerable range, it was a gun of terror. It dealt death to the British in the Revolution, and was decisive in the battle of New Orleans for Andrew Jackson three decades later. It fought the Indians and the French, and it was even copied in England. But principally it was a frontier hunter's rifle, light-loaded for squirrels but with power enough for the slipping whitetail or the black bear shuffling with deceptive speed among the berry bushes. This much power was sufficient for the game available during the period when the Kentucky was at its zenith. The huge buffalo had virtually disappeared from the East (there had never been very many), and the remnants of the Eastern moose and elk populations were in retreat to the north and west.

There were famous builders of Kentucky rifles, working in shops from Pennsylvania through the Carolinas, but some of the finest weapons

Bobcats are important predators and have survived the universal hatred of human generations. Canvasbacks were plentiful in pioneer days, only to approach extinction as drainage and pollution reduced their range. Wolf (below) has almost disappeared from adjoining states, to be replaced by the smaller, more adaptable coyote.

were unsigned. Some were decorated by their owners, and others were the products of several gunsmiths through modification and repair. When the Revolution ended, and the urgency of war subsided, gunsmiths were willing to lend their hands to rococo decoration of patch box, lock, and stock. Curly maple was sometimes burned into striking patterns and brass fittings added. The "golden age" of the long rifle was roughly from 1750 to 1830, when the percussion cap began to replace flint. In the final period of the Kentucky, ornate rifles began to disappear in favor of plainer weapons. By the time the long rifle was modified for western game, it had become less romantic, in appearance at least.

The Kentucky was not, by any means, the only gun in use. The farmer often used a smoothbore musket, loaded with either ball or shot, to shoot ducks and geese on the water and to defend his farm against wolves, bears, lynx, bobcats, and hostile Indians. The long fowling piece, an arm popular in Europe, was owned by the more prosperous settlers. The blunderbuss, a stubby, bell-mouthed, short-range weapon that fired an assortment of missiles and was convenient for stagecoach drivers and horsemen, was never popular in America; it was used more often against human enemies than against game.

The long rifle was an object of pride and it followed that shooting skill was at a premium. Target shooting was an important recreation, and reputations spread rapidly, especially when riflemen were recruited for military service. The famous turkey shoot was conducted in several ways. Sometimes the birds were tethered behind an obstruction, so that only the heads were used as targets. In some contests marksmanship was combined with turkey-calling skill, the heads showing only when the bird's neck was stretched upward; the shooter had to talk his target into position before he could fire. Less dramatic but more precisely measurable was the practice of shooting at an X on a piece of paper.

The accuracy of the rifles varied, as did the shooters' skill, but there is no doubt that an expert could consistently shoot an offhand group of five inches or so at sixty yards. The Kentucky was dangerous to larger targets out to a full two or three hundred yards.

The gray squirrels are busy rummaging in Kentucky's autumn leaves and the hunter can hear them on the forest's floor. He moves slowly—even his moccasined feet are too noisy for a successful stalk—knowing the game is scattering before him, but the long rifle remains in the crook of his left arm. The hunter sees the gouges where squirrels have buried nuts. Several times he sees movement in the high oak branches, but he continues his slow walk until he sights a half-dead monster of a tree, its trunk riddled with holes made by woodpeckers and now usurped by squirrels. In a part of the tree that still lives there is a pair of bulky leaf nests, partly green and partly the red and yellow leaf tones of fall.

There are other nests in the surrounding oaks and the woodsman sits down with his back to a tree, the rifle across his legs with his knees drawn up slightly. The muzzle points upward a little and the toe of the curved buttplate rests on the ground. The right hand rests on the gun lightly, the palm touching the wrist of the stock and the fingers loosely against the trigger guard. He faces forward and only his eyes move as he scans the oaks. It is only a few minutes before he hears rustling somewhere above; it is behind him and he does not change position. A flicker hops in a spiral about the dying tree trunk and the swift, broad shadow of a gliding eagle crosses a sunny spot where a few small oak seedlings are losing a battle for survival to their overshadowing elders.

Untrained ears might not have heard the delicate patter of acorn dust on the leaves. The woodsman, however, shifts almost imperceptibly with the sound, and discerns the grate of busy squirrel teeth seventy feet above. His thumb moves smoothly to the high hammer and brings it back gently, with a pause just before it clicks into its cocked position. The sound is very slight. He has not looked toward his rifle; he searches the high branches until he sees a dark bulge with a trace of lighter outline where sun shines through the squirrel's fur. The sifting of dust ceases and there is a louder sound as the final pieces of the acorn shell are discarded. The woodsman can make out only a part of his quarry's outline, and now that disappears above the limb. Nonetheless, the squirrel's location is plain, for there is a back-lighted fringe of tail fur showing. The rifle muzzle comes up in a steady motion as the stock reaches the marksman's shoulder. His elbows rest on his knees for support. Now he gives a single, crisp bark, a sound often made by squirrels, and the acorn eater's head comes out from above the branch seventy feet up, frozen in watchful curiosity.

The long barrel moves still higher and wavers only slightly before it hangs motionless for an instant and the flint strikes its spark. The report is not loud for the charge is light. It is a sharper sound, however, than that of a smoothbore musket or matchlock—almost a crack—and the squirrel falls straight down. Reloading is swift and without waste motion: the powder quickly measured from the thin-shaved, translucent horn, the neatly patched ball forced down by the hardwood ramrod, and the pan primed. The hunter is back in position.

The second squirrel appears within ten minutes and hops slowly along a small limb of the same tree. This one seems about to jump to another oak but the rifleman stops it with a click as he cocks his rifle and the squirrel's alert pause is fatal. Two squirrels are enough, even for a hungry man who has walked most of the day.

The evening cooking fire is tiny, begun with dry shavings, and its smoke is a wisp that disappears before it reaches the treetops. The long rifle is cleaned and the squirrels are dressed with a few motions and only the tip of the hunting knife. The sky is clear and the hunter makes his pillow of leaves and sleeps fully dressed in his greasy buckskins with a single blanket, deeply soiled and smelling of wood smoke.

At dawn the woodsman washes his stubbled face briefly in a stream that begins as a seep somewhere on the oak ridge. He looks about carefully before he obscures traces of his camp. His ashes are scattered and the bed of his little fire covered with leaves, turned with their weathered sides up.

He is a part of wild America, neither its conqueror nor its victim. His almost shapeless moccasins are adequate for toughened feet. His deerskin trousers and shirt have been copied from the Indians, their fringes designed to lead rainwater away from the wearer. His coonskin cap is a concession to frontier style, the tail left on, and the brass patchbox of his rifle is decorated. His knife sheath and bullet pouch have fringes, and he wears a hatchet with a straight handle—tool, weapon, and emergency knife.

He moves across the high oak ridge to where it breaks away into a valley of small prairies, a hint of much broader ones to come. There is a glint of water at the bottom. The nineteenth century is dawning and he is America's own hunter. He pauses at the edge of his ridge and looks toward the west.

5. Moving West

ameless hunters and trappers first led the way into the wilderness valleys of the West. They had not heard of gold in the Rockies; they had heard only rumors of the Rockies themselves. They had come westward in search of new surroundings and plentiful game. Daniel Boone said in 1799 that the eastern woods had been hunted out. That was not true, of course, but the larger game animals were showing the effects of uncontrolled hunting.

Lewis and Clark formally opened the Far West to the beaver trade yet they were almost to the Continental Divide before they lost the signs of other white adventurers, trappers, and Indian traders who had moved before them by horse, canoe, or bull boat—unheralded silhouettes on the ridges and often unburied and unsought bones in the river bottoms. More than fifty years before the beginning of the Lewis and Clark expedition in 1805, French explorers and voyageurs had reached "the mountains"—probably the Big Horns of northwestern Wyoming. In following the Missouri back to St. Louis in 1806, Lewis and Clark met two American trappers, Joseph Dixon and Forest Hancock, probably the first recorded "mountain men" of the western beaver trapping era. Until the return of the Lewis and Clark expedition, nearly all of the beaver pelts had been acquired through trade with the Indians, but now there began a quiet westward march of white hunters who trapped beaver themselves. It was the beginning of a brief, wild page in American history.

The broad-hatted or fur-capped trapper-hunters of the western plains and mountains were of the same stamp as the long-rifleman of Kentucky. They laid the groundwork for all of the hunters and settlers who came after them. They were independent adventurers with only tenuous allegiance to their government and its rules. They were rebels against civilization, and their trapping in Indian country was against Federal law, although the rule was not enforced. They found uncounted buffalo, deer, and antelope, and they finally met the only truly aggressive game animal in North America—the grizzly bear. It was a perilous encounter. They needed more firepower to bring it down and their demands brought about a new phase in weapons development.

The grizzly lived on both plains and mountains, but generally in rough land, and a century and a half ago it had no enemy to fear, unless an Indian hunting party chose—rashly—to challenge it.

The grizzly became the "great white bear" to Indians who saw its humped, bulky form and silver-tipped hairs against the light. The fur hunters found it much different from the black bears of the East and Midwest, a hazard that often could not be turned by the light-calibered Kentucky rifles. Other wild animals might try to maim or kill under unusual but fairly predictable circumstances; the grizzly could be a deadly adversary at times and places of its own choosing. Only the rattlesnake was as dangerous as the great bear.

In the West, grizzlies were encountered from Mexico to the Arctic, their sizes determined by the food and weather found in their ranges. In the plains country they killed buffalo with shattering blows of their paws. Along the North Pacific coast they fed on salmon through a long season tempered by ocean currents, and became brown monsters that could weigh as much as a draft horse—more than fifteen hundred pounds. Coastal bears not only waded in sloping mountain streams to capture agile salmon with teeth and paws, but feasted on the spent, dead fish after the spawning run had passed.

Opening pages: The Sharps buffalo rifle was tool of sharp-eyed businessmen who pared the gigantic herds nearly to extinction. Their heavy bullets were fired from stands, the gunner resting on a blanket, his rifle steadied in a fork. Skinning knife was broad-bladed and utilitarian. Handloaded ammunition was prepared at night.

The plains and mountain grizzlies of the beaver country were smaller, although a male might weigh more than five hundred pounds. Where winter came early the grizzly hibernated for a longer period and less of its yearly cycle was spent in growing.

In spring the grizzly emerged from its den, its long coat ragged, the new summer hair coming in patchily. It left a trail along slopes of new grass shoots and spring flowers, where patches of old snow still clung. Some of the sow bears were accompanied by new cubs, now playful and fully furred, which had been born during the winter hibernation. There would likely be two or three cubs, and they would not mature until about the tenth year of their twenty-five-year life span.

On the slopes above the willowed draws were the burrows of gophers, also ending their hibernation. The bears found the dens and dug great furrows as they followed the passageways to their prey. As the fugitives were unearthed, the awkward, shambling bear instantly became a quick-striking killer. Excavating methodically, the grizzly moved from one tidbit to another, building strength for the active season, toughening its great paws, and growing fat for another winter. On higher ridges, where hibernation ends later, the rodent prey was marmot. Boulders were overturned and stumps uprooted to get at them, frightening demonstrations of strength for anyone coming upon the freshly scarred landscape.

The grizzly, or the coastal brown bear, is the largest of the world's carnivores after the polar bear of the Arctic. It feeds its muscle with grass grubs, beetles, or carrion, blueberries or venison, and occasionally man. An individual bear may become a manhunter, as might an Indian tiger or African lion. But the grizzly's strength is so superior as to make the tiger and lion seem puny.

Before it learned the danger of rifles, the grizzly met man as an adversary and even hunted him on occasion. It was said the eagle saw the twig fall in the forest, that the deer heard it fall, and that the bear smelled it fall. The grizzly came for miles to dispute the mountain man's roasting buffalo hump or beaver tail. The grizzly destroyed camps in search of food it scented and sometimes it stalked the camper.

There were stories of hundreds of the big bears in small areas, of hunters who killed several in a single day, and of bears which simply denied passage to travelers. When the early trapper rode a horse and was followed by pack animals, the scent or sight of a grizzly could scatter his equipment, supplies, and furs over an entire watershed. Even the truculent boar was less dangerous than a sow with cubs. There was no trail like the grizzly path. It was two tracks, the bear's width keeping right and left paw impressions separated. Other bears following the same route chose the same foot placement, so that a well-used trail might be a well-worn double row of paw-sized depressions, each longer than a moccasin. The big bears left scratch marks high on the tree trunks for the information of other bears. Such ominous signs influenced the selection of campsites.

The mating season comes in late spring and after that males and females go their separate ways. By fall the coats are long and glossy and the bears are at their heaviest. That too is the time when grizzly bearskins are most valuable, but although the fur companies paid good prices, grizzly hunting or trapping was not a way of life. Grizzlies were not sought but encountered, avoided if possible, and hunted only when

*Grizzly bear changed all
hunting concepts, for it was the one
American animal that would
charge without provocation, and the
one whose size and weight
made it invulnerable to the light
rifles used for eastern game.*

it became necessary to rid a trapping area of a constant hazard. In confronting the grizzly with a muzzle-loading rifle, the mountain man had several problems. The bear's very appearance was alarming, for a big male standing on his hind legs could scratch a "bear-tree" trunk twelve feet up. When a hunter first saw it, a bear might well be standing erect, the better to study the strange creature in buckskin with its unusual scent.

Grizzly bears also were unpredictable. There were timid bears, bold bears, hungry bears, combative bears, and even bears with old wounds. The mountain man's gun was marginal at best, and if he fired at long range he lost both accuracy and striking power and might well provoke a charge by wounding nonfatally; on the other hand, at considerable range he might be able to escape the charge of a hurt and bewildered animal and have time to reload hastily for another shot.

If he could approach to closer range, his aim might be more certain, but a charge was quite likely since an instant, one-shot kill was unusual and there would certainly be no time to reload. And at close range the bear would be hard to evade. The grizzly's muscles are enormous and its bone structure heavy, and the slow-moving round ball in use at that time was not overly destructive, even though it penetrated well. There are aiming points which might cause instant kills, but they are small targets. (Expert riflemen of a century later believed the surest way of killing a grizzly was to break both shoulders with the first shot!)

When the grizzly comes he comes fast, long claws tearing the earth for traction, and the muscles bunching hugely under the loose skin. The broad, short head carries the snout forward. The lips are turned back from long teeth in a pig-like grimace. It was not only the ferocity of the grizzly that appalled the mountain men, but the incredible strength which even in the animal's death throes could kill or maim. The unique danger he represented meant that the grizzly's presence in numbers was intolerable—so within a century after Lewis and Clark the big bear became almost extinct in the western states. It was and is a resident of far places, incompatible with the works of man, resentful of his presence and often deadly to his cattle. Today, in the contiguous United States, it survives only in small numbers, mainly in wilderness areas of our national-parks system. Alaska and Canada still support larger populations.

But the grizzly is an individual, and when the mountain man turned a bend in the trail and found himself facing a giant bruin, he could never be sure what might happen next. As he waited apprehensively, flintlock rifle in an uncertain grip, the great bear might roar with rage, flee in terror, or shuffle away with the dignity of a monarch which, for the moment, had no interest in strange creatures smelling of woodsmoke and grease.

It was the thick muscling of grizzly and bison that led to the development of the plains or mountain rifle. Lewis and Clark found grizzlies dying slowly and dangerously with perhaps a dozen rifle wounds, most of them through the lungs. ("These bears being so hard to die," Lewis noted, "rather intimidate us all; I must confess I do not like the gentleman and had rather fight two Indians than one bear.") Their recorded experiences caused travelers to take stock anew of the slender Kentucky rifle with its light caliber and small wrist. The time was near for the transition from flintlock to percussion, the change from pan powder ignited by a spark to the fulminating powder cap, which ignited

*Following pages: The plains rifle
replaced the long Kentucky as hunters and
trappers moved west to confront
dangerous and heavy game. It had a large bore
and heavy barrel, was short
enough for use on horseback. The Hawken
was best-known of several
makes. Most plains guns were sturdy and
functional, bare of decoration.*

with a crack under the hammer and speeded both lock time and reloading. Some of the plains rifles were flintlocks, but the percussion cap was coming into its own. After 1830 it was accepted.

The plains rifle was a modification of the Kentucky. It was shorter, so it could be carried more easily on horseback or on board a crowded keelboat, and the stock was thicker to withstand occasional falls from horse height. Calibers became heavier and graceful beauty gave way to solid utility. Figured woods were largely replaced by plain walnut and hard maple in the trappers' weapons, and plain iron fittings supplanted the brass ornamentation that gave off telltale gleams in the sun. The era of the artistic Kentucky was ending. In over-all appearance the plains rifle showed a return to the style of the European jaeger rifle from which the Kentucky had originally developed. The full-length stock gave way to the half-stock and barrels were usually octagonal and heavy. The gun weighed from nine to fifteen pounds and took extremely heavy charges in soft iron barrels with slowly twisting rifling; calibers went from about .42 to more than .58. The gun's weight absorbed the heavy recoil and aided in careful aiming. It was a forerunner of the commercial buffalo-hunter's rifle.

Kit Carson, Joe Meek, and Jim Bridger all carried plains rifles. Most such guns were made in Pennsylvania (especially in the Lancaster area), in Tennessee, and later in St. Louis, home of the best-known of all—those made by the Hawken brothers. Some of the big rifles could handle more than 200 grains of black powder and a 200-grain round ball. Although the trajectory was a sharp curve that would defeat an unfamiliar shooter, they were accurate and effective up to 300 yards, even a little more. Many were built with set triggers—the forward trigger setting the rear, so that only scant ounces of pressure would fire. (Set triggers had been common on Kentucky rifles.)

It was a formidable firearm and, while it was not positive insurance against the grizzly, it certainly improved the odds.

Even the most inexperienced trapper of 1820 can tell when beaver are plentiful in the valley. In the main river there are fresh chips from their tree cutting, and where eddies have formed there are collections of debris dislodged from incomplete dams. In the eastern foothills of the Rockies, the ridges are dark with conifers, with patches of lighter green where aspen stand. They will turn bright yellow in early fall and become white vertical lines in winter. In the beaver meadows the grass is knee-high during summer, stained by reddened patches of Indian paintbrush and fireweed, and dotted with lacy white wild-celery blossoms. Between the forest edge and the tributary stream, there are trails where moose, elk, and deer travel almost daily. And where one beaver dam of long standing has formed a pond—partly filled with silt and rushes—over an acre of ground, there is a family of Canada geese. Along most of the stream there are intermittent clumps of alders and a few willows. The meadows themselves are formed only where the creek's descent is gentle. There are other sections where it goes down to the river in a series of small falls and noisy, rocky runs.

Along one brushy stretch there are prizes for hungry trappers, a family of young blue grouse walking sedately, on the lookout for grasshoppers in the weeds. They are large birds, almost grown in late summer, and not difficult for careful marksmen to kill. Sometimes they can be collected with a well-aimed stick.

As fall comes on, they will move up the slopes to the conifers. Winter will find them at the end of their short migration, high on wind-cleared ridges, where they will feed on conifer leaves.

It is a new beaver colony that builds its pond in one of the smaller meadows, locating farther upstream from where other beavers have abandoned their lodges after silt and debris gradually filled their little lakes. Old dams have begun to give way and the stream is making a fresh channel for itself. The new pond is located near a miniature forest of alders and only a few yards from a clump of aspen.

The dam is built with a broad base of logs, mud, and sticks, and as it grows and imprisons more of the creek's water, the beavers' task becomes lighter. They have more water for floating logs and have to do less dragging over rocky or muddy ground. By the time the dam is at its full height, their work gives a muddy tinge to the water far below their construction, and even after their pond is formed they continue patching and bracing, until the dam is larger than needed for its task.

The lodge begins in the depths of the pond and grows as a rounded heap, finally emerging from the water and standing several feet above the surface. When there is a nearly solid heap of mud and wood, the beavers begin to cut entrances from near the bottom, eventually digging and cutting a room in the center, somewhat above the water level but approachable only from beneath. They can spend the winter there, their house weatherproofed with frozen mud, snow, and ice, but ventilated near the top where the weaving is not completely tight. Quantities of branches with edible bark are stored in mud at bottom of the pond; they can be reached by a short trip under the ice from one of the lodge's entrances. Within the lodge the beavers are safe from any enemy except man.

In winter the method of the Indian beaver hunters is to chisel through the ice at the lodge's entrance and then dismantle the lodge itself, driving its occupants into a net. In warmer weather they breach the dam to drain the pond, and kill the animals as they clumsily try to escape in the exposed mud of the bottom.

The white trappers blamed Indians for the destruction of both juvenile and mature beavers. The Indians bewailed the coming of the efficient steel trap. But there was a demand for beaver pelts, and there is little doubt that both red and white man used almost any method that would enlarge their catch. The hardship and dangers of beaver hunting left little mood for concern about the beaver's welfare.

The trappers come to the river valley and see the accumulated scraps of gnawed wood in the river's backwater. They have found the drag trails where working beavers have moved their logs, and the fresh stumps where they have felled trees. They hesitate to follow the large stream farther into the mountains, for there are buffalo nearby, often an easier source of meat than deer, and they do not expect to see bison deeper in the forest country. They check the edges of the streams and find the heart-shaped tracks of mule deer and the larger, round-toed trails of elk, and even before they prepare for the fall trapping they have found a sheltered spot for their winter's camp, a time when there will be little hunting and a great deal of cold. Their summer camp is on the river, within walking distance of tributary streams. There are only two men, free trappers, independent of the great fur-gathering combines that send small armies of fur hunters into the Rocky Mountain wilderness—west from St. Louis for the Americans, south from Canada for the English. They have six horses.

One trapper walks into the little valley of the small tributary stream and sees the dam and its muddy pond. It is part of a circuitous route he has planned for his traps, and he carries some of them over his shoulder by their chains, crude and sturdy jaws with long flat springs. He passes the beaver pond and there is a cracking report as a sentry slaps the water with its tail. For a time all is quiet at the pond, and the man continues upstream to where the current is normal again, far enough away from the lodge that a trapped beaver will not cause the colony to leave. Here he steps into the cold water. He does not wince at the shock, for he has done it many times before. (In winter camp his legs will ache because of such wettings.) He wades upstream for a few yards, leaves his rifle on the bank, and goes a bit farther so that his scent will not betray him through dry-ground contact. He comes to a sharp bend in the creek. Not far away there is a wide, muddy path a few feet from the water, a route of the beavers in their quest for saplings.

In the bend the water has dug deeply against one bank. On the other side it shallows abruptly to only a few inches over a gravel bottom. The man carries a sharpened stake and now he reaches into the thigh-deep water to probe for a spot where it can be forced obliquely into the bottom. It goes part way, but he is not satisfied. He finds a boulder he can barely move and laboriously places it on top of his sunken stake, which is now a solid anchor for his trap, with its five-foot chain and swivel. He then sets the trap in inches of water, forcing it down slightly into the gravel so that its trip pan is only a little above the bottom and the jaws are just beneath the surface.

His bait is scent from a bottle, his own concoction involving the castoreum that comes from a beaver's scent glands, and other things to make the substance sticky. He places his "medicine" on one end of a stick and forces the other end into the bottom so that the scent is nearly over the trap. It is on the very edge of deep water, where the inquisitive beaver, attracted by the sign of another animal, will be unable to reach solid footing once the trap has closed and will drown with the weight of the heavy trap and its chain. He retraces his steps and when he has left the stream he makes a small tomahawk blaze on a tree to mark his set.

In another part of the creek there is a sheer bank with beaver holes beneath it. Again he places a stake and stone in deep water, but this time the medicine is put a short way up the vertical bank and the trap is supported by a horsehair and set in a hollowed depression beneath the scent, so that the beaver will reach for footing in order to approach the scent and thus find the trap. He washes the trap thoroughly and scours it with wet sand before placing it. He wishes he could have boiled it, but he hopes the overpowering attraction of his bait mixture will offset any trace of man scent.

In parts of the main river he uses a round bull boat made of buffalo hides stretched, hair-side in, over bent willows almost as large as his wrist. To make the frame, the willows had been cut to the right length and then driven into the ground in a circle, bent together, and lashed at the top. The hides were stretched over them and waterproofed by the application of melted tallow. As the weather grows colder, he and his partner try to avoid wading and use the round boat as much as possible.

As winter closes on the slopes, the beaver are nearly all trapped out in the mountain men's territory. But the trappers have studied a new area

*The wilderness bore the mark of
the industrious beaver, his dams creating
new marshes and eventually
new lakes. His fur drew the mountain men
west, solitary trappers
who blazed the trail for rancher,
lumberman, and homesteader.*

for spring, and they settle down for the coldest months with beaver skins to stretch and flesh, and a store of frozen elk, buffalo, and beaver tail. Their cabin is rough and dirt-floored. Their shaggy horses forage under low tree limbs where snow does not cover the grass too deeply. The valley is closed by snow, and no other man knows where they are; they could not say themselves. But when the snow leaves they will go deeper into the mountains, and they will follow the river down again when spring trapping is done.

The beaver of the mountain men was found over most of America's wilderness from Labrador and Alaska to the present Mexican border. In its northern range the pelts were satisfactory the year around, but in the Southwest most of the trapping of "desert beaver" was carried on only during winter months when fur was thickest. Although there were other uses for beaver fur, it was men's felt hats that used most of it, both in the cities of America and in Europe.

Beavers are monagamous, and mate for life. Mating occurs in late winter, and the average litter is four kits, born over much of the beaver range about April or May. After the birth of the youngsters, the male temporarily becomes a bachelor, often living as a "bank beaver" in a den near deep water, but in autumn he returns to the home lodge and remains with his family until the following year. Young beavers leave home in their second summer, generally mating elsewhere and starting colonies of their own, but sometimes returning to the home pond with their mates. Adults reach a weight of forty pounds, old males even more. The mountain trappers learned the beaver's life story and there were men who returned to the same valleys year after year, carefully regulating their catch so the supply of pelts would be continued. But there were also less scrupulous hunters who decimated the beaver as they went, changing location with each season, a process that penetrated ever farther into the unknown mountains.

The beaver-trapping Rocky Mountain pioneers pursued their primitive careers for only a short while, and if their era can be said to begin with the return of Lewis and Clark in 1806, it was near the end by 1840. By then many of the beaver streams had been depleted, but it was competition from other materials that drove down the price of beaver pelts. Seal, rabbit fur, and nutria from South America had begun to take the place of beaver, and the final blow was the decree of fashion that men's tall hats should be made of silk instead of felt, a decision made practical by extended trade with the Orient. Even before that, settlers had begun to follow the beaver trapper's routes.

Those first routes west stayed close to the old Indian trails. The three major ones were water routes, not that travel had necessarily been by boat or canoe, but because rivers follow natural breaches in rugged country and are certain guides for mapless travelers. Lewis and Clark had followed the Missouri from St. Louis through the Dakotas and Montana, and crossed the Continental Divide to the Columbia River and the Pacific. The more southerly Oregon Trail left the Missouri at the North Platte's mouth, on the present Nebraska-Iowa border, followed it to western Wyoming, where it met the Snake River in Idaho, reaching the Columbia by that route. The Gila Trail left the Missouri at the present site of Kansas City, followed the Kansas River for a short way, then took to the Arkansas for a time to turn south to Santa Fe and the Rio Grande, then to the Gila River across Arizona and to San Diego. Many of the trappers branched their expeditions from these main courses, to be followed by settlers, miners, and finally by railroads and highways.

The trappers traveled by boat, horse, and foot. For most of them it was not a series of annual expeditions from St. Louis, it was a venture of years or a lifetime, and many of them never returned from the West once they took to the Missouri. The mountain man's life span was generally short. He might die at the hands of hostile Indians, as many did, or in a grizzly attack, which was quite common in the earliest days of mountain fur gathering. But the toll of less dramatic destroyers was high. Illness might well mean death where there were no doctors and no medicine. An infected cut or bad bone fracture could be fatal. Many trappers starved to death, for they learned too late there were great expanses where game was nonexistent or very scarce, even in a time of giant herds. They could die of thirst in desert country or freeze in winter, and not all mountain men were equally skilled in charting their movements. Few of them knew their location, having reached it only by a series of stream beds, even though they might be able to return to their starting point. There was a difference between the mountain man and the settler, or even the miner, for the trapper's location was often unknown. In winter the trapper's camp was often completely cut off, even from the trails he used to reach it. Only the prospector of later years approached the lonely self-dependence of the mountain man, and as the era closed there were long but sketchy lists of men who had not been heard of for years. It is likely that the mountain man's occupation was the most dangerous of any in America.

There were very few white women who shared the mountain men's life. Many trappers married Indian women or acquired several squaws who did much of the work about their camps. A large number of the later mountain men were half-breeds. The Canadian trappers were often part French or English and part Indian, and the Canadian trade was handled by both French and English. Many of those who trapped the mountains from St. Louis trails were from Canadian companies, often unwelcome competitors of the eastern firms that bought fur or outfitted their own expeditions.

Even when trappers operated for large companies and made the western trip in a group, it was necessary to scatter widely for the real trapping. Employees of the large companies might go as far into the hills as the "free trappers." Sometimes independent operators banded together for the initial trip west, and then separated into small parties for actual trapping, returning to a large base camp after a season or an entire year of work.

Whatever his independence or his form of employment, the trapper's equipment was much the same. He carried salt, tea or coffee, tobacco, and traps. On some expeditions he carried light trade goods for the Indians. He often had a spare lock for his large-bore rifle and perhaps a hundred pounds of lead and enough powder to make use of it in his particular weapons. Muzzle-loading pistols were part of many outfits. Supplies were supplemented annually at trading posts, at expedition headquarter camps, or at the meetings, or "rendezvous," that became part of the trapping system after 1825.

Originally, the trappers' furs were exchanged at fortified outposts, some of them built by private fur companies, others handled by the Government. The rendezvous changed all that. As much as two years ahead of time, a spot would be selected for all trappers of the region to gather in late spring, to trade

Wagon trains heading west
lived partly off the land, and the sage hen
was available to hunters armed
with crude weapons. Prairie birds and deer
furnished food along the way;
sheep and oxen would be needed at new
homesteads, were too valuable to eat. There
were areas of plentiful game, but there were
many starvation marches as well.

their furs, and to celebrate another year of wilderness survival. Although the meeting might be at some sort of trading-post structure, most of the trappers set up their own camps. The rendezvous brought Indians as well as whites, and trade goods from the East were disposed of at enormous profits. The trappers drank, gambled, raced horses, and fought, sometimes spending the fruits of an entire year's labors within a few days, after which they would begin the long return trip to their beaver streams and solitude. The best-known of the rendezvous were held near the Green River country of Wyoming.

By the time of the mountain men, the Indians of most of the North American continent possessed the white men's firearms, horses, whiskey, and diseases. They, too, made their contributions to the great fur fortunes amassed in the East. Among the Hudson's Bay Company, the North West Company, and John Jacob Astor's Pacific Fur Company, competition was fierce. The St. Louis Missouri Fur Company is another name associated with the frontier trappers; St. Louis was still a fur-buying center a hundred years later.

The keelboat was an important carrier on the Missouri westward from St. Louis. This was a heavy, barge-like, shallow-draft craft with a deep keel that kept it straight as it was towed upstream by men wading the shallows or walking the river banks. It used sails and oars at other times. For years there was enough game along the river's banks to feed the crews and passengers, and the professional hunters were essential parts of all expeditions, ranging some distance from the main route with horses or on foot.

For somewhat lighter traveling there were large buffalo-hide boats, buffalo-hide canoes, dugout canoes, and the cup-shaped bull boats, all of which were readily constructed from materials at hand. Horses

were often acquired from the Indians, and trading goods included guns, whiskey, and ornaments.

Across beaver country were caches of supplies or furs, often raided by Indians, but concealed as well as possible. Many were unearthed long after the beaver heyday—the lost property of dead men. There were friendly Indians and warlike Indians, and small, private wars between trapping factions and the red men. The trapper's warfare was much like the Indian's, for scalp-taking was a trapper custom. The practice had been widely spread if not originated by the whites, since Indian scalps had once brought bounties in the eastern settlements. The mountain man's status was much the same as the Indian's and he often became a member of an Indian tribe, a final break with the civilization he had fled.

The mountain men left little mark. They contributed to the enrichment of fur merchants who never so much as wet a foot in a chill mountain stream. The trails they blazed occasionally were widened and deepened, but where they had trapped the valleys abandoned beaver dams often created silt flats that sometimes turned to grassy ground; other dams rotted and gave way allowing the streams to resume their original courses. In the more inaccessible valleys, beyond the reach of traps, there still were beaver which would multiply and spread.

There is no danger that beavers will become extinct for they can live with civilization if their human neighbors will permit. Sometimes the beaver's busy dam-building becomes a nuisance, and many a riverside property owner has been alarmed to see water creeping across his lawn as the result of some industrious rodent's activities downstream. Beavers have flooded farmland and have ruined trout streams with

their water-warming obstructions. Well into the twentieth century, when their numbers were satisfactory in their natural habitat, they were introduced as a novelty to new areas, even to the man-made badlands of strip mining. In some such places they were welcomed; in others they became impossible neighbors. Use of beaver pelts has risen and fallen in the hundred and fifty years since the first trappers looked behind the ranges, but the animal remains manageable within its habitat.

The hunter walks only a short distance from the creaking wagons and their plodding oxen, and since it is a new land he does not know what to expect. He wants food, not sport, and the travel has been too urgent for him to pursue the buffalo he has seen at a distance, or the pronghorns that have widely circled the wagon train and shown their long, white rump hairs in alarm. He is not equipped for long-range shooting, and although his smoothbore musket can fire a heavy ball if necessary, it is loaded with shot for small game. Once a jackrabbit lopes from its form in the shade of a sage bush and stops to look at him from a little distance, one ear higher than the other as it sits on its haunches, but the hunter decides against firing, for powder and shot are scarce and he has learned that the great, lean hares are tough and skimpy food. He has seen a wolf cross a low rise and a single golden eagle inspecting the settlers' wagons from a height that must reveal, too, the whitening bones of oxen along the deep-cut wagon tracks.

The ground has been rising all day toward a mountain pass. The prairie grasses have becomes more and more broken up by sage and patchy white areas of alkali. Most of the creek beds are dry, but the train is passing one with a few muddy pools in its most deeply eroded parts when the hunter sees something that does not quite fit the pattern of sage, grass, and occasional curved sage roots. It stands almost two feet high and shows above a low bush. When he looks closely, he sees it is a bird's head, almost like that of a vulture from a distance and momentarily quite still.

As the hunter watches, the head moves, the body emerges, and a bulky bird walks forth unhurriedly, at a man's walking pace. A second bird appears, this one going with a waddling gait beside the first, and then both somehow fade into the sage and he wonders if he could have been mistaken. As he moves toward where he last saw them, a bird flies from almost at his feet, the other crouches as if to leave, and he shoots it with his musket. The scarred old firearm must sound as it did long before at a place called Brandywine Creek, but it has been repaired and reworked several times since, and its owner has no notion of its origin.

Lewis and Clark were credited with being the first white men to see the sage grouse, but other travelers undoubtedly had met it without reporting their discovery. Many settlers moving west were surprised by its large size after weeks of seeing sharptails or prairie chickens, and by the comparative ease with which inexperienced shooters could kill it with makeshift guns. It became a staple of frontier diet, and in some settlements it was pickled in brine and stored in barrels against the lean days. The easy shooting that made the sage hen one of the chief targets of early settlers, was later to endanger the species. Hungry homesteaders have different values from those of sportsmen.

The big sage grouse is vulnerable, as is any creature bound to a specific environment with little leeway in food or surroundings. Its home is the climax growth of sage brush and nothing else. From the

Pleistocene era on, there have been sage slopes, usually at fairly high altitudes from 2,000 to 8,000 feet, and they have sometimes spread where heavy grazing has made room for the shrubs in grassland. Elsewhere they have receded as agriculture ate at the edge of native vegetation. It is estimated that more than fifty percent of the sage hen's habitat had been destroyed by the middle of the twentieth century, and there were times when extinction of the big bird seemed likely.

The sage grouse withstands the heat of semidesert country and feeds calmly in screaming blizzards as its nostril flaps hold off the driven snow, but its gizzard is not adequate for a diet of seeds and its staple is sage leaves, without which it disappears. Much sage has been eradicated by projects to encourage the growth of range grasses, and with the disappearance of the sage, the sage grouse and its neighbor, the pronghorn, go with it. The two are together in most of the sage hen's range; in winter the snow-clearing activities of the pronghorn help the grouse's foraging.

The sage grouse has always been a westerner, willing to feed in the settlers' alfalfa fields, or even on green plants that grow in grain stubble. In winter it leaves the deep snows of the higher slopes and goes to the desert ground where the snowfall is lighter. Sometimes it makes limited migrations, flying at eagle's height over the snowy passes. The cocks waddle when they walk; the hens walk straight. When flying, the hen makes twisting turns and the cock holds his course. There is a considerable difference in size between the sexes, the hen weighing about three pounds and the male occasionally weighing as much as seven.

Although the spring strutting grounds of the sage grouse are similar to those of the prairie chicken and the sharp-tailed grouse, the sage hen's size makes it most impressive in the mating ritual. At dawn the birds converge in dozens on the appointed area, each cock holding his chosen plot against invaders, fanning a broad tail, expanding the large air sacs at his breast, and producing plopping or booming sounds. The strutting cock performs many of the maneuvers of the turkey gobbler and is the inspiration for many Indian dances. The strutting area may be the same for generations, and the mating display lasts for much of late winter and spring. At its height there may be strutting at both early morning and evening. The hens observe the exhibition but take little part in it prior to mating.

The sage grouse is easiest to hunt during the late summer and early fall, and there were times in the nineteen-thirties when game managers, fearing the bird's extinction, stopped all hunting in many localities. Adjustments made in open seasons improved the sage grouse's status, but it has stayed near the edge of danger in a delicate ecology, difficult for man to maintain unless the space and sage are there.

Ten years have passed since the Civil War, and buffalo hunting is now a big business, drawing many marksmen to the plains to harvest animals from the seemingly inexhaustible herds. In the camp of one such hunter, there is little activity before the sun is high. The game already has been located and the hunter can wait for the morning grazing to slacken, so the resting animals will be less nervous. The hunter and the skinners sat late by the fire of buffalo chips the night before, loading the long, heavy cartridges, and it is nearly nine o'clock before he mounts his horse and rides to a prairie hill to assess the herd. For several days, he has been working along its borders and he knows the general route of its leisurely grazing. There are no other hunters near, and with care he will fill his wagons with hides in a few days of shooting.

He sees the edge of the scattered herd only a mile from his camp. One of the grazing bands is too large for his purpose, one cannot be reached without passing animals that might take fright, and one group seems restless. Finally, he decides on some fifty that seem to be in an accessible spot and are not too far from what appears to be a good stand, high ground with shallow ravines near its top and fairly tall grass. The buffalo themselves are somewhat below it and probably out of sight of the band nearest them.

He rides to within a few hundred yards of his targets and dismounts, leaving his horse to nibble grass as he walks away carrying a heavy rifle and a few cartridges.

From a distance he studies the lie of the ground and he walks erect for a little way, still out of sight of the buffalo. Then he drops to his knees, adjusts his leather knee pads, and moves a little nearer to the rise. When he reaches a chosen spot he slowly raises his head, but finds he has misjudged. The bison are too close. At that distance the shots would drive them into a stampede. He retraces his steps and approaches from a slightly different angle. This time the nearest animal is an estimated two hundred yards away. He leaves his rifle on the ground and hurries back to his horse for a second rifle and more ammunition. By the time he returns he notes with satisfaction that several of the beasts are lying down and the others are grazing lazily. It is ten o'clock of a fairly quiet morning, and all seem ready for a midday rest.

Like a mechanic laying out his tools for a long and complex task, he puts the sharpened end of a forked stick rest into the ground, spreads a dirty canvas at his elbow, and lays a long row of cartridges on it. He lays his canteen where it can be easily reached and

*Running buffalo was most exciting
of hunting methods and preferred by white
adventurers who imitated the
methods of the mounted plains Indians.
Buffalo-running contests were
common among marksmen who sought frontier fame,
but the tactic was less efficient
than stand shooting. Ideal guns were short
and reloadable on the run.*

places his ramrod and spare rifle on the grass. From this position he can lie prone, with his rifle on a dead rest. He makes an exploratory sweep with its muzzle to see whether he will have to change position if his bison move.

He pours a little water from his canteen into a tin cup, looks about the horizon behind him, and sees the wagons moving slowly toward his tethered horse. The breeze is light and going from the buffalo almost directly toward the rifleman. There is no sign of humans except the hunter's own party. The only ground movement other than the buffalos' is a dark spot that shows briefly on a distant rise and disappears again, a wolf that has taken part in such a performance before and knows to expect good scavenging.

The hunter examines his game, watching for several minutes. Of those still on their feet, one seems to be slightly in advance of the others. Since it is an adult cow he judges it to be a leader. He looks at her over the big rifle's sights, then takes the gun from the rest and smokes the front blade with a match to kill the glare. He checks the range once more to be sure he is not too far off in his estimate, aims, and fires. The gun booms and the blast flattens the grass for a few feet in front of the muzzle. A tiny bloom of dust comes from the cow's side, just back of the shoulder and low, and an instant later the thudding sound of the hit reaches the shooter. Some of the lying buffalo get to their feet at the sound; those near the stricken cow seem more interested in the sudden thud at close range than in the bang and the puff of smoke from a gun two hundred yards away.

There are no wasted motions now as the hunter throws open the breech of the big Sharps and slides a warm, empty case to the piece of canvas a little apart from the loaded ones. He reloads with a practiced motion, searches again with the sights, and nurses the trigger to another shot. The cow he shot stands head down, weaving slightly, but has moved no more than a few feet. Several other animals approach her curiously, smelling fresh blood. One butts her lightly. She crumples to her knees and stretches out. The big bullet has passed through her lower lungs. Now the gun has struck another target; the procedure is much the same. There are four buffalo down and the rifle is hot in the shooter's hands. A single cow begins to walk rapidly, perhaps as confused as the others, but knowing something is wrong. She breaks into a trot and behind her there is a slower movement of animals that begin hesitantly to follow. The hunter swears and calls up all of his self-control to hold and touch off one perfect shot; the new leader drops in a shaggy heap with a big, soft-lead bullet through her neck. The buffalo mill restlessly and crowd together among their fallen numbers.

The rifle is hot and dirty. The shooter reaches for his spare, but that too is hot in a few shots, and he uses some of the water from the cup to wet the rag on his ramrod. He shoves it through one of the bores, then wipes the outside of the barrel. It hisses slightly as the water is applied. The gunner goes back to work.

There are more than thirty buffalo down when the remainder of the band finally begins to move together and break into a run. The hunter swings his sights after them and decides not to fire. They are gone, but it has been a good stand and enough for one day. He waves his hat. The skinners with the wagons and mules start toward the kill. The wagons creak and groan under the growing load of hides. Soon it will be time to return to a main camp. The shooter picks up his empty cases and begins to clean the rifles thoroughly, but first he looks carefully to make sure the firing has not attracted Indians. Before he goes to the wagons he checks the main herd from a higher hill and sees that it is still almost motionless, scattered in endless bands and reaching to the horizon. It seems there are buffalo enough to last forever.

The skinning takes the rest of the day and continues into the evening, but it goes much better than on those occasions when the target band has scattered, or when it had been necessary to snipe animals from a swiftly moving herd. The skinning is dirty business but the men are experts. They do not skin out the heads, and they take the hide from the animals as the Indians do, splitting the skin down the hump. After the deft cuts of the large, curved knife have been made, the hide is stripped off by being attached to a horse. The supper is buffalo tongue, a fare they have liked, become tired of, and then become used to. They say now that it is better than beef. For variety they will eat buffalo hump. Their fire burns buffalo chips and when the prairie turns chill, they sleep under buffalo robes. The wolves cry their wild songs where the carcasses lie, only a little way off.

At the time professionals were hunting buffalo from stands in the eighteen-seventies, demand for buffalo hides was at its height. But the decimated herds were an indication that the harvest of buffalo could henceforth only decline, that the end of the huge buffalo trade was in view. Mostly it was its useful hide that doomed the buffalo, not its value as meat—although this has been a mainstay of trappers and travelers west of the Mississippi and, where transportation allowed, a food item of some importance in the settled areas. From its very inception, the fur trade had included buffalo robes, which made warm bed coverings and protective wraps for passengers in horse-drawn vehicles. The market for them extended from the West to Europe. For almost a century, beginning just before 1800, the commerce in buffalo hides held prime economic importance. It became even greater after 1870, when German tanners perfected a process for turning the hides into satisfactory leather, rather than the soft and spongy early product. With this development, three hundred years of buffalo slaughter reached its peak and the herds entered their last decade of existence. They would have been cleared from the plains anyway. They were incompatible with agriculture, and their destruction was a certain means of controlling the Indians.

Although Indian treaties were almost always ignored, those concerning buffalo country were purposely violated to crush possible hostiles. Some Government officials were frank in stating the situation; others quietly allowed the buffalo hunt to take its course.

Some of the first Spaniards in the West had speared buffalo for sport, and there were occasional hunting trips for amusement by the early trappers, but well into the nineteenth century there were full-scale hunting expeditions in the flamboyant manner and in the European fashion. Sir St. George Gore of Ireland went up the Missouri River from St. Louis in 1855 with forty servants, a hundred and twelve selected horses, milk cows, oxen, more than forty hounds, and a tent of striped green-and-white linen. He was guided by the famous frontiersman, Jim Bridger, and when his party returned in the spring of 1857 they had tallied 2,000 bison, 1,600 deer and elk, and more than 100 bears. They had used heavy wagons and twenty-one two-horse Red River carts, the sort used by hunting parties from Canada. In addition to seventy-five muzzle-loaders and many pistols, Gore took a new Sharps breechloader.

Buffalo slaughter became competitive in some cases, with buffalo runners betting on the outcome of hunts, and when the railroads came out there were hunting excursions in which animals were shot from the train itself. Railroad builders were fed by commercial hunters and their assistants, with buffalo as the principal game. William Cody, who acquired the name of Buffalo Bill, was a professional buffalo hunter for railroad builders and gained fame through contests at bison-running on horseback. In the early seventies, the Grand Duke Alexis of Russia was a guest of American officialdom in a full-scale hunt with General George Custer and Buffalo Bill as escorts.

Buffalo running was sport for many, but it was a less efficient means of collecting hides and meat than the methodical stand shooting. When tanning processes became satisfactory the hunting became truly businesslike, with one expert rifleman serving several wagons with crews of skinners for the hides that would weigh eighty or ninety pounds green. There now developed rifles and shooters that could compare well with those of a hundred years later. The post-Civil War buffalo guns such as the single-shot Sharps, the Springfield, and Remington rolling-block threw heavy, soft-leaded bullets, little affected by winds. A hunter who did his own loading might leave an outfitting point with more than a thousand pounds of lead; he saw special value in a combination of range, velocity, bullet weight, and bullet hardness that would use its energy in the big animal and leave the flattened lead against the hide on the far side of the quarry, where the skinners would find it.

As the boom in buffalo hides reached its height, buffalo hunting attracted adventurers, others who expected market hunting to be sport, and frontier riffraff looking for easy money. A large percentage of the animals was wasted, many of the hides were spoiled through inefficient treatment, and very little of the meat was used at all. The amateurs used all sorts of

*Engulfed by numberless buffalo
eating their way across western prairie,
passengers hasten from Union Pacific
train to shoot what they can. Professional
skinner at left strips valuable
hide from one of day's kill. Carcasses were left
to rot. Photograph shows heap
of 40,000 hides awaiting shipment east
from Fort Dodge, Kansas.*

firearms, but the true professionals chose heavy, big-bore, single-shot rifles for the most part. Some of them used telescopic sights.

The .50-caliber Sharps was an excellent buffalo gun. So was the .50-caliber Springfield. The Remington rolling-block was a sportsman's favorite for many years. Most of the calibers were at least .45, and many expert handloaders found they could safely use heavier charges than their rifles had been intended for. Charges of 100 grains of black powder were not unusual.

Wright Mooar, one of the most successful of the commercial buffalo shooters, often loaded more than 100 grains of powder in cartridges originally intended for considerably less. Many of the old rifles were classified with the bore size written first and the other figure representing the amount of black powder in a standard loading. The Sharps .45/120 fired a 550-grain bullet at 1,400 feet per second and generated 2,390 foot-pounds of energy. The early repeaters, despite their fire-power, used relatively light ammunition and were in disfavor with buffalo professionals for stand shooting. The .44/40, popular caliber of the Winchester Model 1873, fired a 200-grain bullet with 760 foot-pounds of energy.

Some of the early muzzle-loaded plains rifles had power and accuracy rivaling the faster-firing breechloaders used by most buffalo professionals. Their charges went up to more than 200 grains of powder with round balls of about equal weight. Some of the old muskets of .58 caliber used 60 grains of powder and 505-grain bullets. By contrast, the .38-caliber Kentucky rifle, intended for light and medium game, used a ball of about 78 grains.

The marksman must find a compromise between his maximum range and a point from which the game would be frightened by rifle fire. Almost a century after the last of the professional hide hunters had put up his rifle, historians agreed that two hundred yards was perhaps near the average range chosen by the stand shooter, but that he could do well as far out as three hundred yards once he had established the distance.

The abilities of the hard-bitten buffalo shooters are a part of Indian fighting history. War parties were wary of buffalo hunters, or those who knew how to apply the buffalo hunter's tactics under pressure. When possible hostiles were sighted, the experienced plainsman would dismount where he had satisfactory shooting room in all directions, and make the same preparations as on the buffalo stands. Most such encounters ended without shooting and with the Indians riding away. There were some occasions, as at Adobe Walls in Texas, when large numbers of hostiles were defeated by the deadly buffalo guns, which were even more destructive of the warrior's horse than of the warrior. There had been Indian fights there before the buffalo boom, and the hunters and skinners had established a trading post in 1874, when Cheyennes, Comanches, and Kiowas made a concerted attack. Their weapons were so outranged, however, that they retired from the field.

Early in the heyday of hide hunting, Kansas was the scene of the most successful operations, and when those herds faded before the heavy guns of the professionals around 1873, there was a movement southward to the Texas Panhandle, despite a treaty that promised no buffalo hunting in that area. Before 1880 the Texas herds were withering. The commercial hunters went north to southeastern Montana, Wyoming, and the Dakotas. Those herds, ringed by hunting parties of both whites and Indians, were short-lived then, and the winter of 1882-83 was nearly the end of hide hunting.

Much of the work was in caring for the hides after they had been removed. Usually, they were stretched on the ground by use of pegs and a poison applied to prevent insects from destroying them. After a few days of sun and wind, the skins were dry and stiff, and had lost about half of their green weight. In this state they were called "flint hides" and were ready for delivery to a railroad or storage area.

Some of the more businesslike hunters had procedures for salting and smoking large quantities of buffalo meat in the field. At the camps there were drying racks for tongues or other selected cuts. Many buffalo were killed for their tongues only.

In the wake of buffalo hunters came the wolfers, who used poison in the skinned carcasses to kill wolves and coyotes for their hides. The larger kills attracted wolves for considerable distances and it is probable that the prairie-scavenger population reached a high point during the years when the buffalo herds were being destroyed. Most of the big wolves disappeared with the buffalo, although the coyote adapted and spread its range.

By the time the buffalo were so depleted that hunting them was not worthwhile, the prairies were flecked with their bleached bones. There had been some bone-picking while hunting was still under way, but the last remains were valuable enough that organized bone-collection crews sometimes showed more profit than the hunters. Bones presented no problems of preservation, whereas a large share of the hides was lost by spoilage between prairie and final destination. The bone-pickers had no overhead to worry about, except transportation to the nearest railroad. Indians, impoverished by loss of the bison, hauled bones in carts. Even weathered buffalo horns had their value. Although scavenging was low on the social order of the day, it was actually cleaner work than caring for the green hides. There were great ricks of bones piled near the railroads, many of them open to competitive bids from buyers. The bone wagons worked the Kansas plains, then farther south, and so on to the last stand of the bison in the Northwest.

Bones saved many homesteads, as starving sod-breakers encountered scourges of grasshoppers, drought, and blizzards. Like some of the unprepared hunters, many new farmers had come west with a minimum of equipment and knowledge.

New bones were used in sugar-refining processes, and some of the best went into bone china. The old and weathered ones were ground up for fertilizer. The horns were made into knife handles, buttons, combs, and ornaments. For years after the bone gatherers had finished their work the long-sheared sod plows were turning under scattered remnants of the proud "Indian cattle," and then the buffalo was really gone.

In its way, America's bison hunt had elements of the gold crazes and land rushes. There had been killing of both Indians and whites in fights for the herds and the land they used. There had been countless cases of crippling frostbite and frozen death, and, like the mountain man, the buffalo shooter eventually lived out his time.

Now, however sparsely, the entire nation had been spanned by settlers. The beaver and buffalo were no longer important factors, but the settlers saw no end to deer, elk, and the prairie birds—and the market hunters believed their bag would be limited only by their enterprise. They had the guns they needed and the demand for game was limitless.

to Farm

For two hundred years the eastern farmers and builders made no truce with the land. They subdued sections of it and moved westward to new ground. They conquered the forests piecemeal, laboriously cutting the hillside timber; they wore out the shallow soil of their little farms and left to turn fresh sod elsewhere.

The hillside farmers of the eastern states came and went in waves, their fortunes ebbing and flowing with the vagaries of growing industrialism, wars, and political change. From Pilgrim times through much of the twentieth century, hill farms were repeatedly revitalized and abandoned, and many a new farmer found a trace of his predecessors in a broken hoe or forgotten headstone. Those who moved westward to broader fields were replaced by immigrants who clustered in growing cities, and many who left the little farms moved only a few miles to mine or factory. The wooden fences crumbled and the stone fences became green ridges of vine and brush.

Many game animals could not tolerate the settlers. The wolf, an obstinate foe of livestock, disappeared under the pressure of hunting and trapping. The buffalo, believed to have migrated from the gigantic western herds as their numbers overcrowded the range, met the eastern settler's ruthless rifle and hungry family, and was destroyed. The elk, easily found on grassy balds of rounded mountains, was virtually eliminated by 1870 throughout its eastern habitat. In New England the moose survived in secluded bogs, but its numbers were trimmed nearly to extinction. Surviving remnants of the black bear population retreated from the farmer's pig pen to the thickest mountain cover. The panther became a seldom-seen ghost of the farther places and carried a price on its head. The heath hen, near relative of the prairie chicken but confined to more limited range, suffered under the onslaughts of the fowling piece, but vanished only when its habitat was plowed under.

Other game accommodated to clearings and their brushy fringes, and welcomed the abandoned apple orchards. In these places the whitetail deer and the ruffed grouse became true game rather than the easy marks they had been for the crude guns used by the first white hunters.

About 1800, a hunter left his place of business in a New England village and walked to the slopes of an abandoned farm. He carried a long-barreled flintlock fowling piece, not a military weapon, for he had learned to appreciate more graceful workmanship. The game he killed, although important to the family table, was not quite a necessity. The man himself was an outdoorsman, though less weathered than a farmer, and his walks for game were more relaxation than labor.

The ruffed grouse had accepted the abandoned farms and increased its numbers, benefiting from the fact that for more than twenty years after timber is clear-cut and land is broken by the plow there is a succession of plants attractive to him, as well as to deer. It was in the forest edges, along the brushed fence lines and the logging roads that the hunter learned to find the partridge in the fall from New England south through the Carolinas. Later gunners would find them in such cover throughout the Midwest and on to the Pacific Coast as they multiplied in new growth. But the eastern partridge survived.

Grouse mate in early spring after the bristling cocks have drummed atop logs or stones, their ethereal booms echoing across fields and forest. Less than a month after the fluffy chicks have hatched they fly above low bushes and have learned to

*Opening pages: Many elk
originally were plains animals but were
cut off from their historic
migration routes by ranchers' fences and
pushed into high timber. They
adapted to country where hunters could not
find them without difficulty, but
became vulnerable when winter forced them
down to lowlands for forage.*

merge with ground cover when danger appears. In fall the young birds make their crazy flights, probably nature's way of dispersing the brood. It is a mysterious series of blundering trips, nonetheless, and whether the grouse are drunk on fermented fruit or alarmed by wind-whipped autumn leaves is not known, but sometimes the flight ends in a fatal collision with a tree or cottage. It is puzzling behavior peculiar to the ruffed grouse.

By late fall the survivors of a clutch of ten or twelve eggs will have acquired most of their adult cunning. The hunter looks for them near fiery maples, darker oaks, and old apple orchards gone wild, where the forest creeps back slowly in a process that means years of prime grouse habitat. The young fall birds have escaped the weasel, skunk, and raccoon, but will continue to live with threat of goshawk, Cooper's hawk, fox, and bobcat.

In autumn the grouse look for acorns and berries, and have almost forgotten the insects they ate in summer. In winter they will feed on catkins and buds; at one time there were bounty payments for grouse that stripped apple buds too energetically.

There was some commercial hunting and trapping of grouse from Pilgrim days until the late eighteen-hundreds, but the ruff was not so plentiful as the passenger pigeon and not so easily collected as the ill-fated heath hen. Our hunter of 1800 had eaten grouse caught in horsehair snares, but had learned that it was pleasanter to hunt them with his fowling piece. Approaching the orchard of the old farm, he moved cautiously. He stared carefully at the stone fence with its damp crevices and blotched patches of lichens, and when he climbed it he did so hesitantly, as generations of grouse hunters would do afterward, and his thumb stuck out at an awkward angle from his hold on the gun, ready to thrust back the high hammer and its flint.

He has killed many grouse and he hopes to sight them in the old apple trees, but he knows they might be in the brushy undergrowth where they could surprise him. He moves a little awkwardly, so that he will be in position—his left foot well forward—to swing the long gun if a bird appears suddenly. There is one ruffed grouse he never sees. At the orchard's edge it waits in one of the smaller trees until he has passed and then pitches forward from its perch in owl-like silence to slide away behind him into the heavier cover of the second-growth forest, gaining speed as it drops and entering the pattern of shadows without commotion, its wings stroking swiftly yet somehow gently.

The hunter had been aware of other game as he climbed the hill to the orchard. Once there was a very faint whistling sound: an unseen woodcock towering upward through a narrow opening in the branches. The tracks of deer were thick about the old orchard, although at that time of day the animals were bedded farther up the hillside.

As the hunter walks slowly and alertly through the orchard he hears a grouse leave one of the trees, its wings spattering slightly against branches as it somehow escapes without being seen.

He sights no birds sitting in the branches, but finally one roars upward from the ground, its hammering wings trailing a swirl of dust and leaves in the afternoon sunlight. The bird veers behind a tree and then reappears for a moment as it passes on toward safety.

As he hears the first wing strokes and before he sights the bird, the hunter swings upward with his long barrel, the great hammer coming back with the sound of a doorlatch, and the muzzle swishing against

*Ruffed grouse were featured
in game still lifes in nineteenth century.
Shotgunning was a growing sport. The
bobwhite was important game in the Southeast,
where farm practices left field
borders and abandoned land as habitat. Here
pointing dog was helpful
companion. Like the grouse, quail
could live close to man.*

*Mourning doves have been
hunted for a century and seem impervious to
gunning pressure. They have
long been subject of disagreement among
conservationists and sportsmen.
Biologists report that dove mortality rates
are so high that the hunter
has no lasting effect on populations, but
some states prohibit hunting.*

shoulder-high brush tips. It tracks the target blindly as the bird passes the apple tree. Somehow the long barrel has overcome inertia and moves faster as it goes—a fore-shortened, brownish streak to the gunner, pursuing an indistinct brown shadow that seems endlessly ahead of the muzzle. But the muzzle gains and in the instant the bird reaches an open space the gun bangs and a few sun-fringed feathers drift with the gray smoke. The hunter reloads, taking his eyes only briefly from the spot where the bird fell, a spot marked by a swaying bush, and he makes his way quickly to find the dead grouse beneath it. Then, as ruffed grouse hunters have done for three hundred years, he spreads the rounded wings with their flecked brown and gray pattern and fans the broad tail to learn if the black band across it is solid for the cock or broken for the hen.

Even though he now performed an ancient ritual, there was an element of novelty in the kill that gave the hunter particular satisfaction. Sometime, on this occasion or another, he must have decided that henceforth he would shoot no more sitting birds, that this bird and this sport were important enough to have special rules. Wing shooting thus had part of its beginning with him. Not that it had never been done before—but now, as the nineteenth century began, wing shooting was becoming a personal creed. Furthermore, the continuing development of firearms had brought them to a point where "shooting flying," if not easy, was at least practicable. As he walked back toward the village, the hunter may have relived his quick backward sweep of the clacking hammer and the seemingly endless swing of the long barrel. Perhaps he even told himself that the gun was too long and heavy for a true wing shot. Shooting flying, he may have thought, called for something a bit shorter and lighter.

The ruffed grouse, an American bird without close European relatives, had thrived at edge of the forest, then multiplied on the eastern farms and continued to live with man, although its great fluctuations in population remained a puzzle to sportsmen and biologists. It has been called the king of game birds and it has followed as happily in the wake of the chain saw as it followed the Pilgrim's awkward axe—attracted to man's doings yet still a wild bird which cannot thrive on game-farm fare.

At one time the employees of Boston's prominent families stipulated they were to be fed heath hen only "a few times a week." Their protest, like that of other workers who tired of buffalo humps and Atlantic salmon, was a cry of surfeit. The incredible bounty of America was becoming monotonous.

The heath hen's range ran from New England to the Carolinas, favoring sandy scrub-oak plains and some pine sections, and persisting on Long Island long after most of the nearby mainland population had disappeared. By 1850, a long while since servants had complained of too many heath-hen dinners, it was obvious the birds could not compete. Bird lovers, sportsmen, and biologists watched the relentless death of the bird, one of the first extinctions to run its course under watchful eyes and solicitous hands. Like most disappearances it came slowly, in agonizing periods of disease, joyful temporary booms, and crushing losses from severe weather and fire.

There are no more heath hens. They were almost the same as the western prairie chicken, but their home was more restricted and they were unable to adapt when their range was seen to offer ideal sites for pioneer town builders. On the ground the heath hen was a suitable target for the snaphaunce,

and when it rose in flight it often came up slowly and in the open, not too difficult for the flintlock fowling piece and even easier for the breechloader. It did not adapt to man's changes and its habitat was inflexible, so its extinction was inevitable. It was the only native game bird to disappear completely from America.

The heath hen faded rapidly in colonial times, but for a long while it managed to survive, and game managers of a later day spent great effort in nurturing the last colony. They learned the bitter lesson that small, isolated groups of an endangered species are susceptible to localized disasters that would have little effect on a widely-ranged population.

While the ruffed grouse changed from a gawking fool hen to the king of brilliant autumn coverts, the heath hen was only a heath hen, a commodity to be gathered at the outskirts of spreading cities, a bird which stopped at the borders of its traditional range and turned to meet the market gunner's shot. Only a naturalist could distinguish it from the other pinnated grouse which survived in the Midwest and West, but it was important as an example of inexorable extinction. For even though man finally tried to save it, there had been a point of no return, a point that passed unrecognized as it had passed for the saber-toothed tiger and the giant ground sloth long before.

Farther west the prairie chicken dwindled at times, but there was more room for it, and as a result there are huntable quantities in the nineteen-seventies. When the western bird was brought east, however, it could not survive.

The last of the heath hens lived on Martha's Vineyard, off southeastern Massachusetts, for fifty years. In 1890 there were about two hundred of them, and their decline continued despite establishment of a preserve in 1908. They increased briefly, flushing in vulnerable flocks reminiscent of two hundred years before. But during the fall of 1931, the last heath hen disappeared from the scrub-oak flats. Thus the biologists suffered one of their undeniable defeats. And as they watch the few whooping cranes and the desert sheep in their struggles against civilization, they wonder if these species really can be saved, or if extinction has already been ordained.

Extinction came, too, although differently, to the passenger pigeon, nesting and roosting in tree-crushing millions, living its mass existence in some little-understood relationship that doomed its small and scattered flocks once the huge flights had been shattered.

When passenger pigeons migrated from their northern nests, their flocks extended for

*Great gray wolf, a threat
to early American agriculture, was
driven from civilized areas
and replaced by the smaller coyote in most
of its original range. Individual
wolves were able to elude hunters until the
nineteen-twenties, but bounties and
professional trappers banished surviving
packs to wild northern forests.*

miles. Numbering in the millions and flying always in close formation, they actually shadowed the ground. It was said that if the procession curved to pass an obstruction the curve would remain in the flight path of the following birds for hours after the obstacle had been removed. The passenger pigeon was a market bird, captured in fluttering heaps by clap nets and brought raining down by hundreds when shotguns were fired upward at random. The squabs, one or two to a nest, were knocked out with poles. Harvesting was simple, since flocks nested together and might be present in millions.

Dead birds were loaded on wagons, some of them processed on the spot. The last big pigeon nesting at Petoskey, Michigan, was an area estimated at twenty-eight to forty miles long and three to ten miles wide. Before that, the pigeons had changed locations and migration routes repeatedly, their only show of adaptability. From the Michigan kill, barrels of iced birds went to population centers by rail, together with crates of netted live ones. Trees containing up to a hundred nests were cut down and the squabs collected by hand. By 1900 virtually all of the passenger pigeons were gone, either killed for food or doomed by the destruction of their forest habitat. When the killing stopped the remnants never recovered, for their way of life was based on their numbers. No one knows exactly where the last passenger pigeon fell, but that unheralded event became inevitable with the passing of the flocks.

Sportsmen may have vague requirements for a game bird, but nearly all agree it must be an elusive target. Individually, the pigeon may have been that; in its close-order ranks it was not. A game bird must be good to eat, and the pigeon was. A game bird must be hunted instead of simply shot, and it was here the passenger failed dismally, for it came in packed ranks for all to see. A game bird must have strong instinct for concealment and escape; the pigeon lacked these. Perhaps the most sporting shooting of passenger pigeons came when individual birds were released from traps in competitive matches. The passing of the pigeon is lamented, although not by gunners who have pored over the old accounts. They have no wish to hunt it.

In the nineteenth century the forest continued to shrink. The farms spread south, their small fields tilled first by oxen, later by mules and horses, their rail fences harboring weeds and berry bushes that attracted the bobwhite quail. Quail were known along the Atlantic Coast and in the Midwest in Indian times; now the busy seed-eater found new habitat where the forest was cleared and the plow could not reach. He was, as always, an adaptable fellow who could rear his family on a variety of forage. Examination of quail crops has revealed hundreds of kinds of foods in birds that ranged into the northern United States and west to Colorado, but are best-known in the Southeast.

In the South they were aristocratic game to be hunted over leggy pointers in the grand manner, yet also game for the sharecropper's rusty muzzle-loader and his crossbreed dog that slept under a rude porch and shared meals with hounds bred for opossum and raccoon. Those hounds might be the same ones that bayed behind the whitetail deer in river bottoms. At least they were near relatives of the hounds that ran before red coats, musical horns, and tall horses.

The bobwhite quail, with all its qualifications as a game bird, was a renewable resource, responsive to farming practices and quick to multiply when conditions were properly controlled, qualities that led in later years to plantations devoted solely to the welfare of perky birds with humming wings and cheery calls. The quail is important, for like the ruffed grouse it accepted a relationship with farmer and lumberman.

The whitetail is always a resident of the margins, requiring brush and trees for hiding. Although it found new range when the forest fell and second growth arose, its fortunes fluctuated with farming practices and it disappeared in closely settled communities, a victim of the jacklight and hungry settlers. Still, like the quail, it responded promptly to protection and management, as it does today. From the first appearance of second growth until the arrival of the twentieth century, however, its trend was mainly downward.

The whitetail accepted grain or garden as an addition to wild provender, and many a deer fell in the pioneer garden it was raiding, shot mainly for its food value, however, not for its depredations. Many pioneers ate more venison than beef, and when the early settlers placed bounties on wolves it was almost as much to protect the whitetail deer as to protect domestic flocks and herds.

In the West, prairie settlers destroyed the deer. But as their fields divided the rolling lands and the prairie fires ceased, there was new growth in river and creek bottoms, and after nearly a century of absence there were to be whitetails again in the shrubby draws marked by the tallest cottonwoods. From a low point early in the nineteen-hundreds, the whitetail increased under protection and reoccupied many areas from which it had previously disappeared.

In the Midwest and West, the sharp-tailed grouse was an opportunist which had lived well in the grassland, shrubs, and trees. The prairie chicken was more wedded to grass, and although it ate grain, too, it faded where the sharptail prospered. To the rancher both were simply "chickens," and the two birds were freely confused.

No one, whether he studies with binoculars and notebook or simply lives near them in the wild, completely understands the wolf and the coyote. They were and are complex creatures, of so high a level of intelligence that they are strongly individual. Western frontier history is filled with the legends of wolves that lived for years on the edges of herds and flocks, while expert hunters and trappers failed to stop their raids. It was civilization that eliminated ordinary and stupid wolves, and fostered famous and brilliant ones through elimination and selective breeding.

Wolves and coyotes are important in the natural balance of game and predation, and although the sportsman has recognized their value in the wild, the individual sheep rancher or poultryman must be excused for his animosity. A single educated wolf may mean a man's economic failure.

The scientist of the early twentieth century found that the gray wolf showed no hatred toward mankind and even a tendency to friendliness, despite the fables of its ferocity. Their observations make it easier to accept the theory that the first domesticated American dogs developed from wolves.

A carnivore, the gray wolf consumes animals so large that cooperative hunting is necessary. Since the death of a moose or caribou might be a slow and cruel thing, a series of slashing, crippling attacks along a lengthy, blood-stained trail, the wolf became known as a relentless destroyer of living things. When cattle or sheep were substituted for elk or deer, the settlers' hatred of the wolf became a personal thing.

It was the necessity for pack

hunting which made the wolf both spectacular and vulnerable, and forced it to the wildest corners of North America, while the coyote, a small relative that usually sought smaller quarry, could prosper and spread its range. The coyote is not a pack hunter and even in the twentieth century often lives unnoticed in new and closely settled range.

Although true wolves vary greatly in size and color, they have common ancestry and live much the same in the Arctic and sub-Arctic zones as they did in the eastern forests and on midwestern plains. Whether called buffalo wolves, lobo wolves, timber wolves, Arctic wolves, or tundra wolves, there was little differentiation. The smaller red wolf of the Southwest was in danger of extinction by the nineteen-seventies, holding forth mainly in Mexico, and believed by some to be a result of a cross between gray wolf and coyote.

The buffalo wolf followed the great herds, pruning aged, sick, and juvenile bison, as well as antelope and deer—a fanged benefactor contributing to the welfare of its prey by constant elimination of weak and diseased animals. The early wolfers checked the gray hunter's numbers with poison and started his retreat from the grasslands. Those that survived longest were special wolves, students of traps and chemicals, earning individual names and a combination of hatred and respect from harried ranchers and skilled hunters. Usually the famous wolves led packs of their own; even as the packs were decimated and replaced, the leaders held their positions.

The wolf pack is basically a family group, but may include recruits from outside, remnants or offshoots of other hunting clans. The social order is rigid and each member of the pack has his station, difficult to change once it is established, and varying from confident leadership to cowering submission. Lowest is the outcast wolf, crouching scavenger in the track of the killer team.

The size of the pack must be fitted to the hunting. Ideally, it is large enough to pull down game, but small enough to live on the meat available. Perhaps a group of half a dozen is near the ideal number, although really large packs may include twenty individuals or more.

In summer the scope of the hunting wolves is restricted if there are dens of young. In winter the pack's running territory may cover thousands of square miles, or it may trace the caribou's migratory route. Once it would have been the buffalo's course. When the individual pack was trapped or hunted successfully, it was often because of a fatal foraging pattern, so routine that the hunter could anticipate almost the exact night and route on which the wolves would move.

Although a wolf may die under the cow elk's spearing forefeet or the smashing attack of a musk-ox bull, he is ordinarily a match for anything. He may weigh a hundred and seventy pounds and leave a track six inches across. The wolf head is relatively narrower and longer than the coyote's, with a blunter nose and great biting power. Wolf jaws crush bones and shear muscle and tendons. With teeth locked in a moose's great rubbery snout, a wolf may be whirled like a toy, but the fangs will hold.

It is the wolf's nose that finds most game. He is capable of scenting prey or carrion over a distance of miles. When the hunting wolves have located their quarry, they may have chosen it from many large animals by a testing process of short runs to find the sluggish or weakened prey. If hunting has been hard, however, the pack might be forced to choose a healthy

adult and there must be a battle before the feast, sometimes a long and costly one.

∽

The wolves are night hunters and they gather to howl in concert before beginning their tour. It is the most menacing of hunting calls, a sound heard for miles through wilderness darkness. The pack moves over the winter landscape, almost silent, openly crossing the moonlit parks between the conifers. The grass is hidden beneath snow and the forest creeks are nearly silent beneath their icy cover. The wolves are in loose order—traveling to make easy progress—rather than in order of pack status. Simultaneously, several catch the scent of moose. They measure it momentarily in high-headed silence and then dip heads to another level of the scent message. The half-dozen pack members clump in a communication gathering, with nose-touching and the eloquent expressions wolf faces produce, and they change their route directly toward the old bull moose standing quietly in the leafless popple stand.

The old bull has met their kind before. He leaves the trees and pushes his haunches back against snowy bushes, then he faces their circle of excited grins. They pant from anticipation, not fatigue, and they aim their sorties deliberately. Most of the rushes are not pressed home; nonetheless, a flank is soon ripped and a foreleg gashed, and when the moose trots away a short distance—his first mistake in the deadly game—he is cut at ribs and belly. Still, he has no choice but to make another stand.

The wolves are tired, so they alternate their charges. When the bull lies down they harry him to his feet. If hunting had been good they would not have undertaken such a dangerous cause, but they have not eaten for several days. The baiting game continues, although now one wolf limps and holds back. It is a campaign of short retreats and brave stands, and it is many hours later that stiffening wounds and bleeding bring the old bull to his knees for the last time. The wolves feed as their quarry dies, and filled with meat they rest in the snow while a raven croaks in excitement and drifts in for its share. It has followed the pack for a long while, losing it during the night and finding it again after a long, wheeling search from high altitude. Eagles, both bald and golden, might follow the wolves' hunt for remains of the kill. (The great raptors were hunted little as long as the wolf was considered the chief enemy of lambs and poultry; later they would be shot for their share of the blame.)

The pack does not move much for several days. The moose carcass is reduced to a skeleton, then to scattered bones and shreds of hide. Bold ravens, seeking tidbits for themselves, do not seem to mind when the wolves make short rushes at them. They croak in pretended alarm and fly off a few feet, always just out of reach. The wolves wander about without discipline.

When the moose carcass is nearly gone there is a grouping movement of the hunters. One evening they gather with whimpering sounds and much sniffing, and they put their muzzles toward the cold sky and the steam from their howls is a thin haze above them. Then they move off in a loose group. The hunt has begun again.

∽

It was the introduction of domestic livestock that gave the wolf its reputation as a cold-blooded killer, for when the wolf first met phlegmatic cattle and docile sheep it found killing very easy. Some wolves selected only preferred parts of their victims and left nearly intact

*Coyotes widened their range under
pressure while gray wolves retreated. Bull
elk bugles his fall mating
challenges—gouging ground and plants in
his rage—and guards his harem
of cows from other males in mountain parks.
Blocked from traditional
migration routes, wapiti often crowd their
habitat and face starvation.*

bodies instead of scattered bones. Some developed into wanton bloodletters, although others killed only what they could eat. For the most part, it was the compulsive killers that drove small ranchers from their homesteads.

The gray wolf leads his pack about its scent-marked territory, its boundaries plain to wolf noses, and it may take days to travel the perimeter. If there are outlaws in the wild, this band is outlaw, for it feeds on yearling cattle and leaves others dead. It raids the flock of sheep while the herder's eyes smart from peering into the night and his rifle stays cool in his hands, and it leaves a pathetic waste of dead.

The trapper of 1890 knew his wolves. He baited his traps and scented them with rabbit brush and sage to hide any lingering odor of metal. In his cabin a thumbed calendar told the story of wolf raids and spelled the pattern of the outlaw band, a pattern established over a period of months. He knew the wolves' schedule better than they did themselves. He placed his traps—more than a hundred of them—where habit would bring his quarry.

There was a cattle trail where dust easily hid the trap and he herded the livestock well away from it. Along the trail he dragged a dead sheep without touching the carcass by hand. The sheep had been cut to bleed a little, and parts of its viscera were strewn in the dusty path. The man set his traps by approaching the trail from right angles. He had stained his boots in the sheep's blood, and near the traps he used a scent gathered from captive wolves.

When night fell, the wolves, shadowy in the moonlight, followed the drag trail more from curiosity than from hunger. But where the traps were set they detoured; it is impossible to say how they knew the traps were there. They tasted a thousand scents in the slow night air and they found a trace of man smell, perhaps a little also of the man's saddle. Some say they could scent the spots where the drag horse's shod hooves had struck. But no one is sure. It is known only that some wolves have walked around thousands of traps. Certainly the wolves smelled the prepared scent and perhaps they were suspicious because it was so strong. Ever since man had come, wolves had been the hunted as well as the hunters, and their ancestors learned many things in order to survive, while less perceptive wolves died out.

So the pack followed the drag until it caught a change of scent and there in the trail lay the sheep's carcass itself. The pack watched it from a distance for some time. Their chief, perhaps a little larger than the rest but otherwise no different as far as human eyes could tell, was now at the rear of his company. The other wolves formed a rough circle around the carcass and moved their heads up and down for better study of the scent, ears forward and neck ruffs bristling in tension.

To one side and downwind there was a small rise, a mound where some deep rock formation had shoved upward into the nearly level plain. It was a perfect point from which to view the sheep carcass. It was there that a young male wolf went to better view and scent the scene—and, since the trapper knew a great deal about wolves, it was there that the trap leaped and snapped harshly. (Next day, when the trapper found the glossy young dog wolf, it may have snarled and leaped at him, or it may have wagged its tail and lain quietly in the trap, for wolves are individuals.)

The leader of the pack started with the sound of what someone has called the "bright mad steel," but he did not wait long. He left the young wolf in the trap, and he howled once from a hill a quarter-mile away. The young dog wolf did not answer. The leader had seen a wolf die from eating meat with a slightly strange odor, he had seen a wolf caught where the trap leaped from a creek crossing, and another had been trapped at the usual fence crossing—places where the pack now chose new paths. The leader had run at top speed through the dawn across an open hillside and heard the careful, spaced shots from a marksman who knelt by his nervous horse. But he was a bigger wolf than the hunter thought, and farther away, and the well-aimed bullet had gone low, leaving a scar beneath the ribs and a streak where the new hair had grown in white.

None of the original pack was with the leader. They had made mistakes and he was now the oldest of the group. Increasingly he traveled alone, with less trust in the others, and now he had names given to him, names he would never hear, conferred by men who might never have seen him—ranchers and hunters spread over a thousand square miles of plains and hills. Eventually, he would have no pack and would hunt alone, for great wolves often became lone wolves. A wolf became famous through intelligence greater than his fellows' and nearly always through narrow escapes from man in his youth. The famous wolf may have lost a toe in a trap, may have barely survived a taste of poison, may have felt a bullet. If he killed wantonly, many hunters believed it was because of remembered wounds or perhaps the death of a trapped mate. If so, he made the rancher pay, but his kind was doomed and his despised relative, the coyote, multiplied in his former range, no longer fearful of the big wolf's fangs.

The coyote was first known simply as a prairie wolf. Until Lewis and Clark observed it, the white settlers of the East had little knowledge of the animal that was to be America's outstanding example of adaptation to a changing world. Although the average weight of the little wolf might be only thirty pounds, considerably less than that of an English pointer, the coyote's wide head held room for a brain that more than matched the lobo's. Proof was the coyote's ability to thrive after the lobo was gone, living in the same maze of traps, poison, fences, and singing lead.

Lewis and Clark found the coyote west of the Mississippi, from Mexico to British Columbia. Wherever the bigger wolves disappeared, the coyote slipped in on quick feet, and the brittle bark and high wail replaced the deeper howl. In the twentieth century the coyote was seen in almost every state. It followed men, their herds, and their camps, and when the hurrying gold hunters went to Alaska in 1898 the coyote followed and made a home there. When driven from parts of the plains, the coyote took to the mountains, even to timberline and above.

Somewhere in history the coyote acquired a reputation for cowardice, although it is no more furtive than the cougar or the tiger. It dies bravely in pitched battles against packs of hounds twice its size, recovers from terrible wounds that would kill larger beasts, and sometimes robs chicken roost or pigpen in the light of the farmer's window. It has fed on insects, orchard fruits, prickly pear, carrion, mice, high-heeled boots, and a thousand other things, and it learns of new food almost as soon as it appears.

If early accounts are correct, the coyote has changed not only its range but its life style. Once it hunted in large packs, according to the explorers, but today it hunts alone or, occasionally, in very small groups. Except when rearing their young, coyotes seldom live underground, yet some explorers called them "burrowing wolves." Perhaps these customs changed to accommodate civilization and rifles. The coyote is gre-

garious. Groups may gather for a communal howl before a hunt, but the hunt for small game is usually done by individuals, even though there may be frequent meetings and consultations. When scope-sighted rifles are involved there is little safety in numbers.

Coyotes have developed individual hunting traits and, although unable to kill full-grown and healthy cattle, some have been wanton sheep killers, moving into a woolly flock with confidence and deftly slashing dozens of throats. Such killers do not slaughter for food, for no coyote can eat a flock of sheep.

When the chickens and lambs disappeared too regularly, and the hilltop wails and yelps became too frequent, the midwestern farmers held "wolf drives." A midwinter Sunday, after church, was the usual time. There would be a crowd of hunters, and if it was a cold day there would be canvas coats with sheepskin linings and high-buckle overshoes. A few hunters might arrive on horseback but most of the drive would be on foot, for there were generally fences to cross in land long since marked out in mile-square sections.

The hunters would carry shot-guns and no shot would be larger than Number 4, because the end would come at close quarters in a tightening circle. About four of the one-mile sections would make an average drive; at the sound of shots in the air the lines of men cordoned around the area would begin to move. At first the drivers would be more than a hundred yards apart, but as they converged they tightened quickly and noisily. Overhead, a hawk climbed in spirals; the drivers would fire a few shots at it, although usually it was too high. Cottontail rabbits were fair game as they scurried in confusion from fence corners and prairie creeks; they would be supper for the drivers' families.

In the open prairie patches, jackrabbits were killed, too, not for food but for the vaguely defined crime of eating greenery needed for cattle; skunks and opossums might be kept for their fur. But halfway through the drive, and before hunters could see those coming from the opposite direction, the first coyote might be sighted, an alert figure on a spot of high ground, disappearing almost immediately into a shallow, brushy ravine. The word would be passed. As the lines tightened a coyote might run parallel to the row of guns, probing

Coyote sometimes lives in caves dug by other animals and raises young in its adopted home. Bounties are an incentive for hunters to use traps and poison, and to dig young from den after following adult animals to the spot. Coyotes followed miners to Alaska and now occur in nearly every state in the Union despite hunting pressure.

for an escape route but turned back by a spatter of shots and the yells that relayed its direction as it alternately showed on open ground and disappeared in brush.

"Comin' no-o-o-orth!" or "Comin' we-e-e-est!" would roll from man to man, and the shotguns would pop until the closing ring was small enough to make the birdshot deadly and the little wolves would go down from multiple hits, crumpling in silence to the farmers' satisfaction. For the coyote that robs the farmer calls down wrath upon his race, bringing the wolf drive, the Newhouse trap, and the cyanide gun to his fellows, most of whom have done no harm to man.

Yet the hunt was not entirely successful, for some time early in the drive a gray-muzzled coyote, who had seen the closing noose before, ran low and hard along the line. Ignoring stinging pellets and human yells, he chose a gap a little wider than the rest and drove straight for its center, his claws throwing spatters of dirt against the cockle burrs, his gray back bunching and stretching low above the grass and weeds. The two gunners at the gap fired until their guns were empty, but his distance was a little too far.

At evening the coyote stopped on a hill and saw the farmer's house with its yellow square of window, its dark blob of henhouse, and its bulky barn with the pen where there would be suckling pigs in spring, and the coyote lifted his muzzle and howled. There was a trace of caked blood on his side where shot had gone, but that would soon be healed over. The farmer's dog answered in fury, but the caller on the hill waited for something more—another wail from another hill, a long way off, so far that the choppy barks were barely audible after the howl.

Before coyotes became afraid of man they were easily killed with the rancher's lever rifle and occasionally by the farmer's buckshot. But when the bold coyotes disappeared and only the cautious ones remained, new methods of hunting were developed. A shout or a song, it was learned, frequently drew coyote answers which gave a general idea of the animal's location. Sight-running greyhounds and trailing dogs were brought into use, and by the late eighteen-hundreds there were riflemen who could lie still with telescopic sights to watch for the gray shadow on the hill—a sport that became easier as varmint rifles developed.

There had been coyote callers for many years, but only well into the twentieth century was the art perfected and then it became a matter of imitating coyote prey rather than the coyote itself. Usually intended as the squall of an injured rabbit, the call could bring coyotes at a speed which almost overran the concealed caller, day or night. Minor errors in pitch did not seem to matter, perhaps because the call was that of another species. But calling has been a game of sportsmen rather than a ploy in a program of complete elimination.

Poisoning has been a different business. The cyanide gun, which blows a lethal dose into the animal's mouth when it investigates a scented trigger, has killed many curious creatures. And there have been many forms of poison.

Frequently, the coyote has been a valued regulator of more highly esteemed game, destroying the inferior animals. The little fellow's adaptations have included frog hunting, salmon fishing, playing dead, cooperative hunting in which an antelope or deer is run in relays, and duck hunting in which one coyote drives birds to a hidden assistant. And there are demonstrations of coyote gymnastics which draw prey closer out of curiosity. The coyote's basic foods include rabbits and small rodents and its presence can thwart plagues of

*Bull elk resembles stag
of Europe. It was present in eastern
America when first whites arrived,
but soon retired to areas where hunting access
was more difficult, while
eastern habitat was retained by deer and
black bear. Elk were killed
by pioneers on prairie trails but quickly
retreated to high mountain forest.*

either. It is the individual marauder that kills sheep wantonly.

When prairie-dog towns covered thousands of square miles, the coyote was a polished hunter of the rodents. It was even credited with learning to build small wing dams to flood prairie-dog tunnels during prairie cloudbursts. The prairie dog, despite its long-term value in turning over grassland soil, was a short-term destroyer of grass and its holes were traps for running livestock. Poison and sod-breaking plows brought the yipping dogs to a low level. As modern varmint rifles arrived there were shooters in some areas who endeavored to keep the population under control but were careful not to destroy it completely.

There was little migration of big game after white settlement, but such movements had always been short compared to those of birds or fish. The caribou leaves open tundra to spend winter in the forests. Some mule deer come from mountain to valley in time of heavy snows. The bighorn sheep and the elk suffered more from civilization, since many of them were plains residents much of the year, generally going to the heights ahead of the heat and insects. The bighorn became almost entirely a high-country animal within a few years, adapting to year-round residence, but adaptation was more difficult for the elk.

Although wapiti that lived all year on the plains east of the Mississippi had been nearly eliminated by 1865, the livestock industry did not crowd migrating mountain elk until much later. As the Civil War ended, agricultural settlement reached only slightly west of the Mississippi, except for Texas and part of Kansas.

In 1865 and 1866 the really big cattle herds began to move north from Texas to Kansas, competing with buffalo and other prairie game for grass. At first they went east for slaughter, but the drives were later extended to northern grasslands to stock Colorado, Wyoming, Dakota, and Montana.

The nomadic cattle herds of the open range were blocked by the homesteader's crops, and barbed wire came into wide use around 1875, enclosing the cowman's herds and hindering the elk's migrations from the foothills. By 1890 wire-enclosed ranches were established over much of the West.

In summer the elk are scattered in the mountains, grazing along high slopes with forest concealment nearby. The calves, born in late spring, are still leggy and sometimes awkward though capable of bursts of speed in their play.

In early September the bulls begin to sound their mating challenges, each with his distinctive tones of wild whistle and belligerent grunts—the heavy-antlered herd bulls confident, and deep-voiced, timorous youngsters faltering and sometimes failing to produce a whistle at all. The harems are gathered, their masters presiding with menacing fury and false charges against weaker challengers, and now and then there is a grunting, earth-gouging battle.

With September come the early snows and most of the warfare is suspended as the large flakes fall. The big bulls rest where they can watch their cows, their backs matted with snow and their antlers outlined in white. They are in their winter coats and when the late summer snows melt they may bed in the last thawing patches.

As the rut subsides the bulls forget their romantic differences and begin to group together, often a little apart from cows and calves. Though

at night there are hard freezes, it is not yet time to go down the mountain. Some of the high meadows have several inches of snow which a band of elk must brush aside to reach the grass, leaving snow in furrows.

When heavy mountain storms finally arrive the herds drift downward, sometimes grazing and browsing as they go, moving in single file where there is little for them to eat. The bands have their individual wintering ranges, valleys and foothills where only the most general storms bring heavy snow and where they can find willow cover in time of blizzards.

Early in the nineteenth century there were elk that lived their entire lives on the plains, but they were too vulnerable. Immobilized in heavy snows, they were even clubbed to death in the winter of 1855-56 in Greene County, Iowa, with men, women, and children joining in the pursuit. The last elk disappeared from the New York hills about 1850, from Pennsylvania about 1870, and from West Virginia slightly later. By 1870 the plains elk were scarce and the mountain elk were under siege.

The mountain elk had to change their ways or perish when they found the ranchers' fences across their downward routes. Several hundred pounds of elk can smash a fence easily, and a band of hungry travelers had little to fear from domestic cattle about the stacks of alfalfa—so the rancher declared war, reluctantly in some cases because he may have held his precarious homestead by virtue of years of elk steaks, but by 1910 the elk's numbers were at low ebb.

Best known of the migratory elk routes were those of the Yellowstone National Park/Jackson Hole herd. They summered in the high country and some wintered in Idaho at the north end of the Teton Range. Others went to the willow bottoms of Wyoming's Green River and in especially severe winters traveled as far as the Red Desert of southern Wyoming. There were reliable reports of cows and calves there in 1868.

It was a slow process, first this canyon and then that slope blocked by settlement, but it was a universal process and it gradually stopped the longer migrations. It reduced elk numbers, for high summer range could not support animals with no recourse to lower altitudes in winter.

But there were narrow routes where the elk continued their annual travels and the hunter knew them. It was partly sport and partly a harvest of meat. The hunter worked upward until he was near the migratory trail, and after several days of watching he would find the procession coming down across the talus slopes and steep faces in single file, grazing a little where the ridges were blown clean, then moving steadily ahead of an advancing storm.

In the Wyoming mountains the hunter found his spot and chose a boulder as a rest for the heavy octagon barrel, its weight padded by his extended hand. He peered carefully through the high tang peep sight and over the rolling-block breech and fired his heavy, soft-lead bullet through the first snowflakes. It struck the lead animal back of the shoulder, and there was a clatter of loose rock and a brief crashing of timber as the herd scattered. The prize was a fat cow, and the hunter went back for his pack-horse.

Once he reached the cow the hunter probably noted she was a bit older than he had hoped, though there was still a great deal of prime meat. There was no outward difference in the appearance of the cow from that of others in the herd, but it was she who had carried the secret of the trail to the valley grass where the winter winds touched lightly. She had learned it through several trips, traveling first as a calf, and eventually she would have passed it on to younger elk. Now the band she had led lacked a leader for the winter trip. It would stay in the mountains to browse the saplings high and strip the aspen bark above the reach of smaller, cold-weakened animals. The band would starve down and become smaller, stabilizing to fit a range that must serve both winter and summer.

The pattern of reduced migrations continued and even in mid-twentieth century there was crowded mountain range. Elk drifted downward to open valleys and their herds were trimmed by firing lines of shooters who protected the valley ranches. In the nineteen-fifties riflemen still stopped elk at the borders of Yellowstone National Park. Turned back, the elk continued to outgrow their range at times, and destruction and transplanting were tried to prevent near-total starvation. Then a public that could not understand winter starvation, that had seen fat animals on lush summer pastures, opposed killing and preached that bales of hay could take the place of valley pastures.

The elk, filled with a vitality that drives it to travel with injuries that would cause a moose to crumple, can nevertheless become an indigent waiter for hay trucks, a tame and slothful pensioner who refuses to forage for himself.

Thus the wild and resourceful bugler of the wilderness becomes a farm animal, and a steady diet of man-served hay allows a herd to outgrow its range completely. Living in a concentrated community for which it was never intended, the animal becomes diseased and weak. At the outset of the nineteen-seventies, managers of elk herds decided to undertake feeding only as an emergency measure, to be done in such a way as not to foster domestication.

There are special strains of elk, such as the Roosevelt elk of the North Pacific rain forests and the small tule elk of California. The latter is a capsule of twentieth-century elk problems, an animal endangered by over-zealous attention in a limited area and a subject of friction between managers and preservationists. The tule elk, reduced to such small numbers that hunting was not practicable, was relegated to a small area where forage matched the herd, but protectionists demanded a larger number so game managers sought new places for them to be introduced. There was no suitable room in California.

The elk was always highly respected game. When it left the East to be welcomed in the mountain states, it became a controversial figure. Men wanted to keep the elk but they wanted it on their own terms. They found it an efficient competitor of beef so they fenced it from the plains and deserts and blocked its routes to the valleys. In the wilderness it was an elusive quarry, yet it could be a smasher of fences, a gorer of livestock, a render of haystacks, and a sharp-hoofed slasher of farm dogs. It has been an animal of much respect, but it is no gray squirrel to be hidden in a woodlot until hunting season. When a creamy bull with towering antlers is trapped in a stockade to reduce the crowd on tattered winter range, there are few elk lovers who want him alive in such conditions.

This is one of the great American game animals, now living in some of the most colorful and most difficult of hunting terrain. It is outsized for small-scale wilderness and it cannot live in fence corners. Any elk that dwells close to man must become a domestic and thus it loses the qualities that riflemen value. The elk hunter, remembering cold dawns, laboring packtrains, and high-country camps, is not cheered by elk in zoos.

7. Meat for Money.

Game for Sport

For America, the thirty years beginning in 1870 were its "golden age of hunting." Never again will there be so much game. Never again will there be American hunters with so much field experience, and the professional shooter will never again have the prominence he then enjoyed.

The champions of that other century still are remembered by Americans who know nothing of current marksmen, but somehow feel that Doc Carver, Annie Oakley, William Cody, Adam Bogardus, and Fred Kimble will never be equaled, even with today's improved weapons. The old champions killed upland game by the barrel, and waterfowl by the wagonload instead of by the sparse legal limit. The professional buffalo hunter killed by the thousand. His descendants seek a single trophy.

The market hunter sometimes combined sport with business, and he was not easily classified. He might have been a poor, lazy squatter who lived in a shack at edge of a river or a forest and sold game to feed his family. He could have been an energetic businessman who did his gunning efficiently, with careful attention to marketing and shipping, perhaps a combination of dealer and shooter. He might have been a marksman who simply sold wagonloads of waterfowl or prairie chickens to defray his hunting expenses.

The methods of the market hunter were much like those of the wealthy sportsman whose private railroad car sat on a siding near the game, and who counted his kill by the thousands. When the first rich gunners of the eighteen-hundreds traveled west to Illinois, Ohio, or the Rockies, their expeditions involved transportation through unsettled Indian country at great expense and with a small army of guides, domestics, wagoners, and grooms. Railroads opened the western game country to sportsmen and market hunters of more modest means, and the golden age of hunting dawned. Its dates are somewhat vague, but it began shortly after the Civil War and ended some time early in the twentieth century. It was a period when game hung by the ton in city markets, and ranged from meadowlarks and plover to venison and waterfowl.

There were attempts at conservation, but most of the public saw game as an unlimited resource, a harvest that required no planting and came free with the nation's millions of virgin acres, and miles of coastal and inland waters.

The harvest was not necessarily easy. On the Atlantic Coast the wildfowler's days and nights during the great flights were cold, wet, and dangerous ordeals. The shooting day of the eighteen-seventies began with no hint of dawn and the treacherous sinkbox was an unwieldly tow in a black wind that brought the deep-water ducks low and restless over the rough salt water. The box was hardly a boat, although it floated, almost submerged, with wings that spread flat on the surface to break the waves.

On the wings were iron decoys. Handmade wooden ones were set in the water by the hundreds, so that from a little distance the arrangement would appear to be an island of rafted ducks. The gunner lay nearly flat in his coffin-like chamber, where spray and sometimes solid water crossed the wings. Downwind, a boatman waited for the kill and the cripples.

The shooter ballasted his "battery" with stones, so that it stayed low in the water, swinging downwind from its anchor, and if the wind suddenly became too high he jettisoned his ballast and anchor to drift until picked up by the attending boat, or until he grounded on shore. As he waited for the game

*Opening pages: Using large-bore
shotguns, hunters of the "Golden Age"
gathered enormous bags of geese, ducks, and
upland birds. Railroads took
city sportsmen into game country and market
gunners used the rails for delivery.
Until refrigerator cars were developed,
however, much game spoiled
during warm weather for lack of ice.*

to tip down over his decoys he lay with his head slightly raised and his long, heavy shotgun resting with its muzzle on the footboard of his box. He might kill five hundred ducks in a single day, and although his firing was restricted to a small angle directly ahead, the decoys were arranged so that the birds he sought came to the target zone almost with certainty, their paddle feet down, their airspeed failing, and their wings cupped as they reached for water, attention momentarily fastened to their landing spot rather than the wooden decoys or the battery itself. And that was the precise moment—as they were almost motionless over the water, but coming down in a crowd. There was a little downward momentum to slow their escape and the canvasback's bullet body and wind-splitting head were no help. His hissing speed could not be regained in the split second between the two booms of black powder.

Celery-fed canvasbacks and redheads were most valued in the city markets, and when the supply began to fail they became gourmet fare, brought from Chesapeake Bay or Currituck Sound, with the canvasback costing as much as $7 per pair by 1890. The bluebills, or "broadbills," were less highly valued.

A hundred years after the heyday of Currituck Sound gunning there were stilted blinds by the dozen on the reedy, brackish expanse, and guides still hosted shooters from eastern cities, but the day's bag was unlikely to be more than three or four birds, and canvasbacks and redheads were not to be had. Some birds the hunters killed would have been scorned by the old market shooters.

But some of the traditions remained, and in 1970 there were stored ricks of handmade wooden decoys, some of them the property of two or three generations. A few craftsmen still made them by hand

to be bought by local guides who scorned newer designs of plastic, rubber, or cork, and insisted the wooden blocks were worth their extra cost. The makers, often older men who had heard of the greatest days from their fathers, complained that they could not keep up with their orders and could find no worthy assistants.

Wooden decoys had been popular since about 1800. The outsized blocks of the twentieth century were little used in market days. Some of the old decoys were built with high-held heads to avoid icing up in rough water; ice on beak and head could cause an unnatural float. Later builders avoided the high head since it is typical of nervous birds. The market shooters ignored such niceties, for removing ice from more than a hundred decoys might be a grueling and time-consuming task.

In the golden age, punt guns of huge bore were used for some commercial shooting. They were very nearly cannons in size, and mounted on sneak boats which usually were manned by a team of hunters. One sculled from a reclining position, while the gunner directed him from the bow with foot nudges and handled the gun, which was usually mounted on a swivel. He often fired just as a raft of ducks rose from the water, so that they would be as much exposed as possible, the great charge of shot plowing a gap in the rising birds. Lighter guns were used to dispose of cripples.

But some of the most deadly of the market hunters fired from blinds much as are used today, using decoys or simply pass shooting along known flyways. On inland waters there were expert human callers, as well as live decoys, of which most shooters used only a few, together with wooden imitations. Live decoys were nearly always mallards, and the "English call" ducks were a small and noisy breed of mallards, three or four hens doing enough calling for the largest passing

Deep-water ducks were killed
by market hunters over huge decoy sets.
Artist depicts Canada-goose
blind along shoreline with gunner using two
shotguns. Prone gunner sculls
a duckboat with punt gun mounted in bow.
Lighter shotgun is inside boat
to dispose of cripples, and push pole is kept
for fast shallow-water travel.

WILD FOWL SHOOTING.

H. Drake

flocks. The term "stool," as applied to decoy sets, came from the small pedestals used to rest live birds. There was a ruse of hiding live mallard hens at points some distance from a shore blind so that they would gabble constantly with each other and thus attract airborne flocks. Drakes are less voluble and call weakly.

It was pass shooting that demanded the greatest skills of waterfowlers, and the vast numbers of birds produced experts whose feats could not be duplicated in later years, simply because hunters who came after the great flights had little opportunity for so much long-range shooting. It was the waterfowlers who first felt the need of better shotguns. One of them became the best-known of the market wildfowlers and was credited with development of the shotgun choke. Though others had worked with barrel constriction before his time, Fred Kimble proved its worth and brought it to efficiency in America.

Kimble, who hunted ducks along the Illinois River, experimented with choke boring and came forth with a muzzle-loader that greatly extended his range. A 9-gauge piece became a Kimble favorite, even surpassing twentieth-century guns in patterning. His muzzle-loader, using Number 3 shot in its large bore, was not handicapped by forcing cones, the constrictions just ahead of the cartridge in modern breechloaders. Thus there was little deformation of the shot, and Kimble, one of the great competitive shooters as well as a hunter, had the ability to swing the tight pattern with accuracy. He was credited with killing more than fifty passing ducks in succession without a miss.

Pass shooting is done when the birds are in full flight and often at long range, requiring a fine judgment of distance, target course, and bird speed. It must be a well-timed swing that sends the charge to the point where the bird will intersect it. The master gunner's mathematics is a personal thing with little relation to ballistic computations. Fred Kimble's leads were estimated from bird lengths, but the speed at which he moved the muzzles of his guns could not be described to student shooters, even though Kimble was one of the most articulate of the market gunners. A hundred years later there were a few great pass shooters who had learned to shoot as youngsters before the flights had thinned. Most of them are gone, but the marksmanship of men like Nash Buckingham was admired in the nineteen-sixties by those who had practiced mainly on clay targets.

There had been breech-loading shotguns of a sort since about 1850, but in the early seventies they had not been accepted by all hunters and the objections were valid. At that time the breech-loading hunter loaded his own shells and might fire so many in a day's shooting that they were almost too heavy a load to carry. They were usually made of brass, for the first paper cartridges were fragile and could be ruined by water. Although breech-loading was faster in the field, a user of the newer guns might spend the night loading shells while his muzzle-loading companions slept. And as breech-loading became more common it competed with advanced methods of muzzle charging. Some muzzle-loader users carried a few small metal tubes loaded with shot and wads, already measured and ready to be put into the bore. The tubes could be recharged when shooting was slow. And muzzle-loader charges could be adjusted to immediate field conditions.

Preferred shotgun bores of the late nineteenth century averaged considerably larger than those of later smokeless-powder guns. The early waterfowl hunters along the East Coast felt that 10-gauge

Today's hunters seek waterfowl
in reduced marsh habitat, and legal limit is
small. Ducks and geese are most
difficult of management tasks, migrating over long
routes that present a variety
of hazards. Federal regulations seek fair
hunting seasons for all states
along flyways linking northern nesting sites
to subtropical winter quarters.

*Waterfowl hunters used
large boats disguised with greenery
for drifting to ducks on
the water. Their targets were resting
birds as well as those in
flight. Numbers of waterfowl appeared
endless, and hunters
understood little of their migration
routes or destinations.*

was too small and preferred 8-gauge or larger until improved ammunition changed their minds. Duck and goose guns were very heavy. Although bulky black-powder charges were used, the amount of shot was often no greater than that in modern smokeless ammunition in smaller bores. Current labeling of smokeless ammunition follows the old custom of marking shot cartridges with the powder charge's equivalent in drams of black powder. A modern 10-gauge magnum load throwing two ounces of shot, or even a 12-gauge magnum with $1\frac{7}{8}$ ounces, would compare favorably with the charges used in guns carried in the field in 1880. Some of the punt guns, of course, were more heavily loaded, and a man in a sinkbox might use a twenty-pound weapon with extremely destructive charges. But Adam Bogardus, competing in a glass-ball match in the eighties, used only $1\frac{1}{2}$ ounces of Number 8 shot in his 10-gauge.

Until a New York State Sportsmen's convention in 1872, the various shot manufacturers had individual designations for shot sizes and the figures meant very little. Specifications were adopted at the convention and there was some conformation, but it was a long while before true standardization came about.

Perhaps some of the Bogardus preferences on shot and shotguns reflected the opinions of the time—or molded them because of his shooting fame. His preference in an all-round gun was a ten-pound, 10-gauge double with 32-inch barrels. He used less shot in breechloaders than in muzzle-loaders. He felt seven to seven and one-half pounds was the minimum for shotgun weight and advised the purchaser to choose the heavier gun when in doubt.

For prairie chicken he used only an ounce of Number 6 shot. For forest grouse he used nines in the early season, then went to eights and sevens as the birds became wilder and more heavily feathered. His quail loads were eights or nines and he went to tens for snipe. For the most part, the upland hunters of that day chose slightly smaller shot (at least in designation) than used now.

Bogardus believed the smaller shot had greater penetration, a premise of some shooters today, especially when duck down is involved. However, his belief that it had more velocity (published in his book of 1899) has since been disproved.

Joseph W. Long in *American Wildfowl Shooting* (1879) said the 10-gauge should use 1 to 1¼ ounces of shot with up to 5½ drams of powder. An 8-gauge, he said, should weigh at least twelve pounds and should fire 1½ ounces of shot (the standard charge for a modern 12-gauge short magnum cartridge).

The trend was toward smaller bores and lighter guns as ammunition improved. The 12 became the standard shotgun, and now is being challenged by the 20.

American-made rifles had served the frontier and the early sportsman, but for many years it was the English shotgun with its artistic lines and meticulous workmanship that was most sought by American sportsmen. The British maker, using simple tools and skills passed down through generations of craftsmen, stood at the bench his father had used and shaped guns from rough blocks of steel and billets of cured wood. From such benches came the Boss, Purdey, Greener, Holland and Holland, Westley Richards, and the other great British guns, some of them obscure as to name but secure in their designation as among the finest man can build.

Then came the breech-loading American double guns, built at first in a compromise between the Englishman's timeless handwork and what was one day to be mass production. These were the Parker, Fox, Ithaca, L. C. Smith, Lefever, and Baker, some of them merely sound, practical arms, and others near-perfection, resulting from files and chisels that would not hurry, a school of gunmaking almost gone today. Over a period of one hundred years the fine American shotguns came and then nearly disappeared, but the old names returned in the nineteen-seventies, when an affluent society asked for close tolerances and high polish. It was the general popularity of hunting among shooters of modern means that eventually brought the efficient repeater with its interchangeable parts, a development that drew imprecations from lovers of English guns, and really began with Eli Whitney's concept of mass assemblage.

It was typical of American development that the famous Parker shotguns began as part of a line of merchandise produced by an early industrialist, rather than as the idea of a lone genius in a tiny shop. The first Parker shotgun was developed in 1865, when the Meriden Manufacturing Company changed from Civil War armament to sporting guns. It was a breechloader, the barrels were of Damascus steel, and it competed for a time with muzzle-loaders. It endured with modernization until 1947, a career similar to that of other fine American double guns, and like most of the others it was discontinued in the face of an economy that had little place for a maker who moved precisely and used only a file.

The repeating shotgun was beginning to take its place as the century ended and it became an American institution.

∽

There were some game birds that dwindled in numbers during the golden age and were later completely pro-

GROUSE SHOOTING.

*Rail shooting of Golden Age was
done with light guns and poled skiff. Early
shooters wore tall hats
to be seen over vegetation. Pushers
charged "by the tide," and
shooting was easy enough for beginners since
all rail are slow and awkward
fliers. Steady operation of the boat is most
important in aiding gunner to hit.*

165

tected by game laws. Most of the shorebirds and the plovers, some of which were upland rather than marsh dwellers, were removed from hunting lists by the time of World War II. Of the small waders, only Wilson's snipe was a game bird in the nineteen-seventies. During the late nineteenth century the golden plover visited the midwestern plains by millions. They preferred closely grazed fields and congregated in glistening, wheeling clouds where freshly burned prairie had begun to renew its growth with green shoots.

The plover gunner often wore neutral clothing, much as the wildfowler did, but he seldom used a blind. He often lay on the ground until a flight came within range, and studied flock movements to find the proper spot. Then there was the method of buggy or wagon hunting, and there were gunners who used a single horse with specially built gunning sulkies carrying a box for game and shells behind the seat. Plover that flushed too soon if a man walked toward them would allow a team to be driven nearer, and the driver would go briskly as if intending to pass the birds, then stop suddenly and alight to fire. He might make the same approach with a saddle horse. It was a hunting trick that had worked for centuries and still works, the hunter approaching at an angle instead of directly, appearing about to pass the game by accident.

The stalking horse took hunters near to a variety of ducks, geese, and shorebirds, and required little training, possibly carrying the shooter and his weapon to the general area and then serving as a moving blind for birds accustomed to the random wanderings of grazing livestock. The gunner sometimes used a short length of stick with a snap fastened to a bridle bit, and he walked with his horse between him and the game, steering it with the stick. If his horse permitted it,

he might fire his first shot under the animal's neck before the game flushed. There were refinements of the procedure and two shooters could use the same horse if it were properly trained.

Along the shore the tolling dog would bounce playfully, chase its tail, and roll over, a strange and unexplained attraction to deep-water waterfowl which raised their heads in curiosity and cautiously swam closer. The busy dog would not cease his gymnastics, but his antics would take him ever closer to a blind at water's edge. The waterfowl, obeying impulses that have ruled them for centuries, approached the guns in a compact and nervous mass. The tolling dog was a tool of both market and sports hunter, and he did with training what his wolf and coyote relatives had long done through instinct when they brought swimming ducks within range of attack by an associate crouched in cattails or bulrushes. There were tolling dogs bred for the purpose, but any breed might be trained for the task.

Shorebirds were a commercial delicacy, and the one that survived the market hunting days to remain a game bird for at least another hundred years was the Wilson's or jacksnipe, a will-o'-the-wisp of bogs from Alaska to Florida. Some snipe nest above the Arctic Circle, making southward migrations by stages, difficult to predict even for seasoned hunters. But in the market-hunting era they came in weaving, twittering swarms that bunched and divided like undecided bees. A "walk" of snipe was a compact mass resting on a muddy flat, birds to be harvested by a heavy, raking charge of fine shot.

The snipe wades, but not deeply, and its chosen feeding ground is mud with a glaze of water that usually shines in the proper light, and as the gunners swung heavy shotguns at the twisting targets

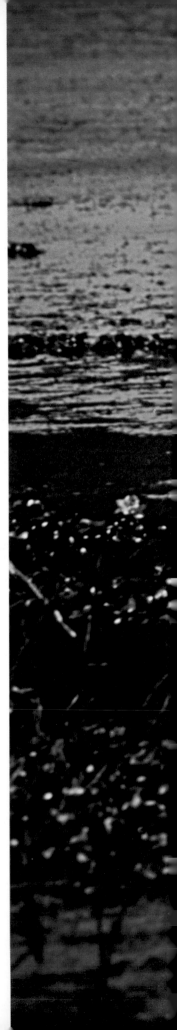

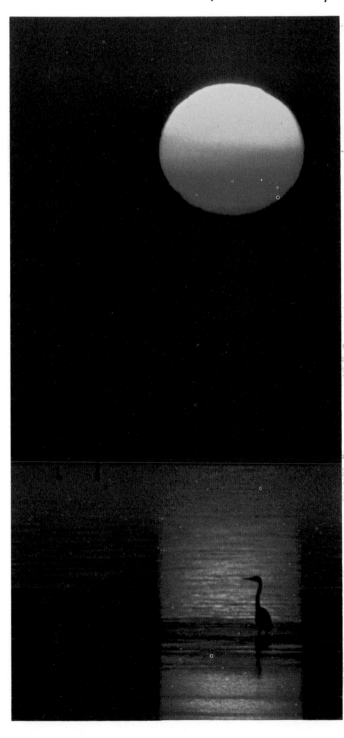

*Marsh hunters are watched by
great blue herons, residents of shallow water
over much of United States and
silent fishermen of the edges. Common egret
(far right) wades southern marsh past
water-hyacinth raft bordering the land.
Large wading birds were killed
as game during this prolific period, when
size of kill was most important.*

Shorebirds were prized game
of Golden Age of American gunning, hunted
over handmade decoys. Seasons
were closed due to game shortages, and only
Wilson's-snipe shooting was resumed
after World War II. Beautifully finished and weathered
decoys became valued collector's
items, representing craftsmanship of bygone years and
gunning days gone forever.

they began to accept this bird as a challenge to marksmanship. They tallied their kills and percentages of hits, while they polished shooting techniques and studied the bird's flight pattern to better their scores.

The snipe is primarily a worm feeder, leaving probe holes and white splashes similar to the woodcock's, but preferring somewhat wetter ground. Its legs are longer and stronger than the woodcock's. As the supplies of other waders were depleted the snipe continued to thrive because it lived in more difficult terrain, often flushing from bogs that required strenuous wading by hunters. The deep mud that can hold a few ounces of snipe on its surface is a morass for the gunner. Snipe decoys were much used around 1900, generally placed on mud banks where there was little vegetation, and giving a clear view to passing flocks. The shooting was from blinds. Some of the decoys were simple cutouts but others were carefully carved, each imitation supported by a single, pencil-like wooden leg stuck in the mud. Snipe decoys fell into disuse as the birds became scarcer. When snipe shooting was legalized again after World War II, following a long closed period, there was hardly any decoy shooting, and the old wooden imitations became collector's prizes.

Snipe hunters preferred to walk downwind so that flushing birds would show their light undersides as they took off upwind. Birds that flew close to the brownish marsh vegetation were difficult to see unless the gunner caught a glimpse of the nearly white belly. Despite a habit of calling "scaipe!" as they flushed, many snipe were out of range before they could be located. Parties of shooters often drove flights of birds toward each other. In areas where shooting pressure had been mild, snipe would swing back over the shooters for a closer look, giving difficult shots. Spring shooting was easiest because the birds were heavier and slower then.

Like snipe and waterfowl, the ruffed grouse was a special challenge to the sport gunner of 1870 because it was a difficult target. The bobwhite quail was sometimes netted but was usually shot singly, and thus it appealed more to gentlemen sportsmen than to full-time commercial shooters. In arid areas of the West the valley quail was hunted commercially by shooters hidden at waterholes, and the birds gathered in immense flocks to be shot on the ground. The prairie chicken of the Midwest was a game of moderate difficulty, usually hunted with wagons and often with pointing dogs. Early morning and late evening were most productive, since the birds fed in open fields at those times and usually spent midday in heavier cover of weeds or brush.

By the late eighteen-hundreds pointing dogs were highly valued and had been in use to some extent for more than a century. English pointers and setters were best known. Flushing spaniels were in use, and there were many waterfowl retrievers. It was much later before a variety of "new" European pointing breeds became popular in America.

The shorebirds were not the only game that lost the sportsman's interest as their numbers declined. Rails and gallinules, often referred to simply as "marsh hens," were prominent in city markets and offered easy wing shooting from poled boats, requiring no great efficiency with firearms. Marsh-hen shooters and polers often wore high hats so they would be more visible to other gunners working their way among tall reeds. The rails are slow fliers and often simply skim the water or the tops of the reeds in short flights.

The sportsman might perch on a stool as his poler moved him gently along a maze of

*Remington rolling-block and
Winchester Model 73 were
top rifles of Golden Age. In
short model, rolling-block
was an efficient saddle carbine.
Model 73 was provided as
a musket for military use with
full-length stock. Sharps
Creedmoor rifle (right) is
carefully checkered
competition model with
precision sights to
handle long-range targets.*

Virginia rail is a common member
of a class of wading and swimming birds known
as "marsh hens," which includes
gallinules as well as several species of rails.
Marsh hens are not strong
fliers and are often difficult to flush for
their short flights. In coastal
marshes they are most easily found at high tide
while feeding among reeds.

water trails, paths formed naturally or by boat traffic. His gun was open-bored and loaded with small shot. At high tide, game might be either swimming or standing on patches of fallen vegetation as it fed in brackish water. (Many rails were shot "sitting" by commercial hunters.) The boat was slim to penetrate the reeds, and the gunner could easily miss if his platform was unsteady at the crucial moment. If he hunted for sport it was often a problem to make the game fly. When his poler called "Mark right!" the shooter would turn quickly but smoothly, to humor the skittish boat, and catch the bird as it cleared the reeds—a difficult shot for a right-handed shooter. The poler would mark the exact location of the fallen bird and maneuver for the pickup. Another rail, flushing to the left in a water-flailing escape, would swing the gunner quickly to his natural side, but if the moving skiff tipped slightly against a clump of matted vegetation as his trigger finger tightened, the shot very likely would chop harmlessly at the reeds. Marsh-hen shooting can be a game of balance and position. It has never attracted a large number of practitioners.

The large wading birds, such as sandhill and whooping cranes, were popular market game, hunted with decoys or in pass shooting, sometimes bagged on goose or duck hunts. Immigrant workers killed thousands of songbirds near the large cities, using inexpensive guns, and small birds were found in many markets.

Those who defended market hunting declared that there could be no final shortage of game, and that unused game was wasted, and they insisted that the commercial kill was well used. But spoilage was the specter of the market gunner far from customers and refrigeration, and he often accepted it as a normal part of his overhead.

Ice was precious in the market-hunting areas. It was cut from lakes and rivers in winter and stored in ice houses during warm weather. When game was shipped, ice took up much of the space and increased shipping weight. In the field it was seldom available, and the problem was complicated by year-round hunting. Prairie chickens were especially vulnerable to spoilage since they were usually carried to railheads or steamer landings by wagon, piled so that body heat and late-summer temperatures combined to ruin the meat; as summer birds they were soft fleshed, anyway. After transportation by wagon in the hot sun the game was then bagged or shoved into barrels for long rail or steamer travel with or without ice. Waterfowl suffered almost as badly, although they were usually killed nearer to rail or ship transport.

But tastes in game have changed greatly since 1900, and much that appeared in city markets then would today be considered completely spoiled. Aging was a part of game preparation, but it was carried to great lengths through necessity, and the palates of nineteenth-century Americans were adjusted to it. Much winged game was simply thrown away before it could be used, just as tons of buffalo meat were wasted. Even when dressed immediately, big game such as buffalo or moose could spoil easily in warm weather. Body heat is sufficient to cause souring unless the heavy shoulder sections are separated promptly, even if the rest of the field dressing is completed. It took hours to dress the harvest from a successful buffalo stand.

Winged game and other birds suffered year-round sport hunting and market shooting and then, as the century closed, there was a new hazard: a craze for feathers, bird skins, and stuffed birds as feminine decoration. Hardly any sort of bird escaped the feather hunter. Hummingbird and songbird skins were placed on hats; often the entire bird was suspended over the hat crown. Plumes or feathers came from cranes or eagles, as well as from lesser victims; but it was the tropical and subtropical birds that suffered most. For the first time the southern swamps were abused by commercial shooters.

Wading species of the Everglades roosted and nested in rookeries, a single roost often accommodating egrets, herons, storks, spoonbills, pelicans, white ibis, cormorants, and wood ibis. By day the rookery was quiet, with only a few nesting or loafing birds present at all times, but the ragged trees showed the wear of thousands of crowding bird feet. It was to such sanctuaries that the hunter came.

In late afternoon the shooters reached the rookery island by boat. It was only two acres of mangrove trees set in shallow water at the edge of the Gulf of Mexico, off Florida's southern tip. The tangled roots and mud of the island were heavily matted with years of bird droppings. Weather was calm, ideal for normal bird movements, and the shooters' skiff was drawn into concealment among low mangrove bushes. The men stood knee-deep and a little apart from each other, each within shotgun range of several large mangrove branches that had lost most of their leaves to bird use.

An hour before sunset there was bird movement toward the roost, individuals and pairs slowly flying in leisurely inspection of other islands, some of them stopping along the shores where a trace of water movement indicated tiny fish, or that the tide level was right for oyster-bar inspection. A little later the flights came in uneven lines against pink thunderheads, and moved urgently as night closed. They dropped to the

trees without ceremony and jostled each other with petulant squawks. The various species were grouped together for the most part, but small flocks of each kind were scattered over the entire island.

The shooters began firing before dusk, shooting when groups of valuable birds assembled, so that shot charges would be most efficient. The egrets were most desirable, but others fell as well, almost any feathers being of some value. The men gathered their kill by torchlight. They might come again another night and shoot the roosts by the light of torches or lanterns, or on another occasion, if the tree arrangement was right, they would use nets.

The plume and feather hunters were not sportsmen, but ruthless destroyers, especially when they killed the adult egrets at nesting time. The plumage is at its best then. In a way, the slaughter of birds for their feathers was the beginning of the end for large-scale commercial hunting, because the results were flaunted constantly from women's hats, and public sentiment eventually turned against the practice. The Audubon Society campaigned forcefully, and prominent women were ridiculed for wearing plumes. The Lacey Bill, introduced by Rep. John

Lacey of Iowa, and passed in 1900, prohibited interstate commerce in feathers and skins. There was some illegal plume selling after the act became law, but fashion changed and artificial flowers largely replaced feathers.

As the nineteenth century ended, sportsmen's organizations became involved in enforcement of game laws and sued restaurants that served illegal game. There was hardly any Government machinery for game-law enforcement, and game management was in its infancy. Most local laws of the time were aimed solely at excessive market hunting. The public attitude supported the right of individuals to kill any amount of game at any time for personal use.

The buffalo slaughter ended midway in the golden age. The deer population neared its lowest point in the East around 1900. All big game of the plains was greatly reduced. Transportation difficulties protected high-mountain animals, such as sheep, goats, and bear, but trophy hunting was beginning and outfitters met their clients at the railroads.

It was a time of rapid development for big-game rifles. The buffalo hunters led the way in the use of accurate and powerful weapons, such as the single-shot Sharps and the Remington rolling-block, both of which threw heavy, soft-lead bullets with extreme accuracy, but with a looping trajectory that made fine range judgment essential. The repeaters had been under development since before the Civil War, but they used lighter loads and were essentially short-range arms.

When American riflery was challenged in 1873 by an Irish team that had won the championship of the British Isles, it was with specially built and tuned Sharps and Remingtons that the Americans were able to win. The match was fired at the Creedmoor range on Long Island, built by the new American Rifle Association. "Creedmoor" models were the finest of American target rifles up to that time, and they became collector's items of great value. The Remington rolling-block competed with later designs and was manufactured until 1933. Target rifles were equipped with the finest of adjustable sights, and although telescopic sights were used by some buffalo hunters, it was after 1900 that they became popular.

The Henry and Spencer lever-actions had been used during the Civil War, and there were levered repeaters of one sort or another for many years prior to that. Immediately after the war the trend in lever-actions was toward higher velocity and smaller bullets. Marlin, Winchester, and Savage became well-known names as the century ended. Although the bolt action of the twentieth century was basically stronger, simpler, and more accurate, the lever action retained a large following and the bolt was considered slow and awkward.

The Winchester lever Model (of) 1873 was a considerable improvement over previous repeaters, but it owed much of its popularity to the .44/40 cartridge which worked both in the rifle and in heavy revolvers. Use of the same ammunition in rifle and side-arm was a great convenience to hunters in primitive areas. As metals were improved and actions strengthened, some lever-actions began to use larger cartridges. Theodore Roosevelt used heavy-calibered lever-actions and killed the largest of African game with the Winchester Model 1895, using the largest cartridges available for it. This model was popular in .405 caliber and a 300-grain bullet, with which it was used on the heaviest of game. Modern rifles seldom use heavier than 300-grain bullets for American hunting although bullets of more than 500 grains are commonly used at short ranges in Africa. The

Model 1895 was at one time chambered for the .30/06 military cartridge, thus moving into truly modern ammunition.

Until the introduction of smokeless powder in the eighteen-eighties and nineties there were definite restrictions on bullet velocity. Killing power was mainly a property of bullet weight, and "flat-shooting" weapons were unknown. Bullet expansion was moderate and only soft lead would "open" at all. Hard jackets were unnecessary for slow-moving hunting projectiles.

Black powder is bulky, burns with a great deal of residue, requires frequent cleaning, and is comparatively inflexible as to speed of burning. Smokeless powder can be made in endless variations of burning speed and is adaptable to a wide variety of cartridge sizes and bullet weights. The French Lebel 8mm was the first smokeless-powder centerfire cartridge and was developed in 1886, followed closely by Germany's 8 x 57 Mauser in 1888, and the U.S. Army's .30/40 Krag in 1893. Now that metals could handle the high pressures of smokeless powder, the quest for velocity as an aid to accuracy and killing power began in earnest. Hunting bullets were soon developed for the military cartridges, but the bolt action was slow to find a prominent place in the game fields.

The high-velocity revolution for hunting rifles began with the .30/30 in the Winchester lever-action Model 1894 rifle and it remains the most popular of all cartridges for close-range medium game in the eastern United States, a reign of eighty years.

The hunter was glorified during the golden age. Proficiency with firearms acquired a charisma never reached before or since, and showmanship was at its peak. William F. Cody became Buffalo Bill to the world when he was selected as a perfect example of the outdoorsman by E. Z. C. Judson, writing as Ned Buntline. Cody was a fine hunter and excellent shot, but it was his showmanship that glamorized the marksman. He was twenty-three-years old in 1869 when Judson chose him as the hero for hundreds of stories of the Wild West. Cody brought his guns to vaudeville and the circus, and the era of the exhibition shooter began.

Competitive shooting was not well organized and targets were not standardized. Many of the early competitions were largely a matter of endurance, and in some cases the targets were fairly easy. Target rifles had a long way to go, but by 1880 the great wing shots had shotguns that did nearly as well as weapons of much later. Some of the early competitions were actually matters of hunting, Fred Kimble and other market shooters betting on their skill in duck blinds or on the prairies. Most of the experts had killed thousands of upland birds or waterfowl. Newspapers carried the challenges of local champions who wanted to compete with other shooters in the game fields.

The live-pigeon shooting match had become popular in Britain shortly after 1800. Birds were placed in holes in the ground, covered by old hats, and the shooters were ready to fire when the hats were pulled away and the birds took flight. Then came a variety of traps which released the birds when a cord was pulled, the origin of the "pull" command of modern clay-target shooting.

By the early seventies live-pigeon contests were popular in America. At first the targets were passenger pigeons, but as those became scarce common domestic pigeons were used; they are still used in American live-pigeon shoots where they are legal. British shooters used a faster-flying bird, native to their country, and American competitors who went abroad for their sport had difficulty adjusting to the more agile flights. A variety of other birds, including sparrows and starlings, were used as targets; bats proved difficult to hit, but hard to find in sufficient quantity.

Glass balls were popular in exhibition shooting and were used in competition through much of the golden age, some of them filled with feathers or other materials to make a hit more spectacular. George Ligowsky of Cincinnati patented a clay pigeon in 1880 and this type of target rapidly replaced metal, glass, and cardboard. Later, clay gradually gave way through experimentation and the present composition is largely dependent upon pitch, but the term "clay target" remained.

Adam H. Bogardus, hunter, author of hunting literature, and powerful demonstrator of marathon shooting skills, was possibly the most widely recognized "world champion" of the time, but W. F. (Doc) Carver was one of his constant competitors and the two engaged in a series of exhibition matches. Carver had a show of his own before Cody entered the business and was later a part of the Cody Wild West Show. Late in his shooting career he performed high-speed aerial shooting with a Spencer pumpgun.

In competitive shotgun shooting, Carver, Bogardus, and Fred Kimble enjoyed equal reputations, although Kimble did less campaigning and used less showmanship. The best known of all the great shooters was Annie Oakley, who gave exhibitions over much of the world and was an attraction with the Cody show. Her husband, Frank Butler, was also a famous marksman.

The end of the century began a gradual decline in public enthusiasm for great gunners. More sophisticated entertainment gradually replaced trick shooting. The "wild West" had grown tame.

8. Adjustments in

the Wild

hadows are deepening while the quail hunter loads his wagon. He has only a short distance to go, and already has put in a full day's work. He calls himself a brushpatcher and his equipment bears him out. His short, light shotgun is marred by scratches and his canvas trousers have innumerable small tears where briars and branches have gouged them.

Only one dog rides with him in his station wagon, a veteran pointer with somewhat tattered ears and a few scars of his trade on legs and sides. The pointer's social status is above dog boxes and he occupies the rear seat in dignity, scorning the bouncing enthusiasm of less experienced campaigners, but giving a restrained whimper now and then.

The destination is only a little past the edge of town, where small housing developments are still new, some of them having usurped old orange groves. There are neat lawns where the hunter once tramped with his present dog's grandfather, and promising clearings in brushy sections beyond the houses.

He parks the station wagon at the edge of a small field grown to weeds. There are partridge peas, a section of broom sedge, and the remains of an old grove along one side, evidence of some destructive freeze of years ago. His hunting ground is near the northern border of Florida's citrus belt and the time is 1965. For years quail hunters have complained that the birds have changed and become addicted to running instead of holding close for pointing dogs, as the bobwhite is supposed to. They say that there is some strain of pale Mexican quail, introduced long ago—a kind of quail that runs instead of flies. They say there is a special breed of swamp quail that refuses to come into the open and is darker in color than the other birds. They say, also, that the quail population is down because modern practices

have allowed the brush to become too heavy.

Most southern quail hunters prefer hard-running dogs that cover great open spaces with flash, and they watch them go from the high seats of vehicles built for the purpose. Their hunts are day-long affairs, covering miles, and they regret that their hunting areas are reduced by development and no-trespassing signs, many of them posted because vehicles have made hard-packed roads across pastures, even through productive groves. Many such hunters have sought private leases for their sport, adding their own posters to those of the farmers.

The brushpatch gunner puts his dog down where the small field merges into brambles and palmetto. There are tall oaks with sweeping Spanish moss only a little way back. He carries his gun at high port, for he expects only quick chances at birds, and his dog works slowly and very near the brush, which seems impenetrable at first glance. There is a spot only a few yards from the field's edge where the weeds are thin, and there are several little depressions where birds have dusted recently. Older pockets show the effect of rain. Very near the brush he finds the little circular patch of droppings where birds have roosted in weeds thick enough to give concealment, but open enough to allow sudden flight.

It is only a few minutes before the pointer slows his busy quartering and works his tail violently. He moves to the very edge of the heavy cover and stops there to look toward his master. They both know that birds have run into the brush and that there will be no open shot. The hunter turns into the brambles only a few feet behind his dog, holding his gun in one hand and fending off the clinging vegetation with an uplifted arm. His heavy shirtsleeve shows the wear of other such trips and his snakeproof boots feel for footing as he

*Opening pages: A band of bighorn
sheep moves across a high pasture in the Rockies.
Bighorn receded from early range,
are now being put back where habitat permits.
Below: Moose have splayed feet
for travel on marshy ground but are no match for
snowshoes when drifts are deep.
Old illustration shows shooter about to bag
plodding game in dead of winter.*

*Wilderness pack strings take the
hunter into roadless mountain country for big game.
Cougar is wariest of American game,
often living unseen near humans. It is an
important predator of deer and
culls inferior animals from herds. Winter range
is critical for elk. Herds confined
to high country must be regulated or their food
supply may be permanently depleted.*

moves slowly to where a rusty barbed-wire fence makes his progress even more complicated.

Fifty yards into the tangle the dog stops in a point, but his head moves uncertainly and he takes a few tentative steps on a mat of oak leaves. He waits for the hunter, and then the quail give away their presence with small twitterings and some guttural clucks never heard by quail gunners who find their birds either frozen in hiding or humming in flight. The covey's feet patter on the dry leaves and the brush patch is quiet again as they stop in indecision.

The gunner moves to one side in hope that he will cut off the birds, and he hears some of them move again, then stop. He stands still, hearing a whisper of breeze in the Spanish moss and conscious of the dull roar of a nearby freeway. Then a pair of birds flushes somewhere, the sound of wings mingling with a rattle of small branches and leaves, but he cannot see them except for a shadow that crosses up ahead. He waits tensely, the silence wearing at the scattered covey's nerves. In a moment, a single cock leaps upward, almost at his feet, and flies hard across a small opening, tracked by the ready gun. The shot is muffled in the brush and the target falls, together with branches and leaves, making a light thud somewhere in the tangle of bushes. The dog hunts for the downed game, his snuffling loud in the dull light, and the other birds fly off unseen.

The hunter seldom collects a limit on his afternoon expeditions, but he has adapted to a situation, even as the quail have adapted. It is not a new kind of quail; the birds have changed to fit their environment. Quail that live in the open have fallen to more conventional hunting methods, and it may be a short-term evolution that has produced the brushpatch runners. No amount of planting can renew the open-country birds.

Because the bobwhite can be raised in captivity, and because quail can increase their numbers quickly when conditions are right, the bird is a capsule example of the complexities of American game management. A profession of the twentieth century, game management has been an outgrowth of an oversimplified program of protection that began with the premise that game would multiply if hunting stopped and propagation was encouraged. It was a long while before game was recognized as a renewable resource that could not be stockpiled.

The quail hatchery was once believed the solution to quail numbers, and millions of dollars were spent in efforts at increasing populations which already filled their habitat. Although it remains a valuable tool in case of natural disaster to breeding stocks, and can give a quick start to newly prepared range, the hatchery cannot produce a bumper crop where nature rules otherwise. By the nineteen-thirties biologists saw the error of unregulated introductions beyond the carrying capacity of game ranges, but even forty years later there were hunters who found their game depleted and cried for plantings of new stock. It was not that their game had been hunted out, but simply that conditions had changed, and the land could not support more. Spectacular results from introductions of birds and animals in special cases made the situation more complex and difficult to explain. With modern management the problem became more and more one of habitat and less one of breeding stock. The disastrous results of overcrowding were hardly considered until the nineteentwenties. The fact that one hundred deer would starve where fifty could prosper took a long time to prove.

When most of the eastern deer

populations reached an all-time low shortly after 1900, there were few sportsmen who believed there could be a comeback. Then commercial hunting was reduced, law enforcement was bolstered, and a few introductions were made in good habitat that had lost its game. In Pennsylvania, where it was believed the whitetail was gone for good, deer multiplied rapidly after a few introductions, and their prosperity was aided by new growth following timber cutting. Preserve areas offered complete protection in some regions.

Having saved the whitetail from oblivion, man failed in his role as a predator and indulged in overprotection, believing it impossible to have too many deer. The buck-only law was a mainstay of early conservation but became the cause of disastrous crowding. In the nineteen-twenties sportsmen remained militantly opposed to doe killing, despite the recommendations of game managers. By the mid-thirties, deer were starving. The average size of Pennsylvania deer had become smaller, winter kills were heavy, and the herd was in real danger. Then seasons on antlerless deer were accepted and the population was finally stabilized.

Similar situations occurred in Wisconsin and Michigan, and overpopulation was common in western states. Residents who loved to see herds of mule or whitetail deer during summer drives in the country were not present when starving animals crowded into snowbound yards in winter and browsed the vegetation until it took years to recover. By about 1960, most states were "on top of the deer situation," and managers believed they could maintain healthy herds. Their constant fight was against the popular belief that reduced kills and artificial feeding were perfect solutions to all deer problems. Although it has been worthwhile as an emergency measure with both deer and elk, feeding

can easily bring overcrowding when the balance is delicate. Most sportsmen are horrified to learn of a "good winter kill," even though it is an essential tool of nature.

The Kaibab deer explosion of northern Arizona is a much-worn subject of conservationists, but it was more than a simple case of overpopulation. It was an observable example of overpreservation, predator-game relationships, and all-round nature meddling. It has served biologists as a text for fifty years, and exemplifies most of the general principles of management.

The Kaibab Plateau was set aside by President Theodore Roosevelt in 1906 as a game preserve. It was excellent mule-deer range and supported about three thousand of the animals at a time when all American deer were in desperate straits. Government hunters moved in to destroy cougars, wolves, coyotes, and bobcats, thus eliminating a major safety valve of the population. There was no deer hunting, so the fanged predators were not replaced by riflemen. The livestock that had been using the area under Federal permit were greatly reduced. But what had appeared as a wondrous garden spot of nature became a disaster. By 1922 there were at least 20,000 deer. (Some believed the total reached 100,000.) With the destruction of nearly all deer food, including cliff rose, aspens, and other browse, starvation decimated the herd. A limited hunting season failed to reduce the excess, and a band of cowboys, encouraged by Zane Grey, novelist- outdoorsman, also failed in an effort to herd the deer to new quarters.

Political friction between Federal and state authorities hampered relief, and antihunting forces steadfastly opposed any kind of harvest. Finally, hunting helped to stabilize the remnants of the herd, and the habitat began the long road to recovery, but not before complex political realignments had ponderously

Following pages: Pronghorn of western prairies is the swiftest of American animals. It has returned to huntable numbers from near-extinction, with modern game management protecting surviving herds and restocking animals in sections where they had disappeared. The pronghorn is capable of living in overgrazed land and now resides mainly in sage country.

accepted practical management procedures.

The pronghorn came back from dangerous scarcity, much as the whitetail deer did, and these are the two best examples of managed recovery among big-game animals. (They are called "medium game" by many hunters.) It has been estimated that there were sixty million pronghorns in the early nineteenth century. Their tan and white multitudes appeared as "moving hills." They lived then with buffalo herds much as they later lived with domestic livestock. From the eighteen-fifties through the eighties they were hunted commercially. A great many hides were shipped east and pronghorn meat was sold in San Francisco.

During settlement of the West pronghorns were killed for a variety of reasons other than for the market. Settlers used them for meat. Cattle and sheep ranchers believed they were range competitors of livestock and slaughtered them in large numbers. The antelope's habit of feeding and resting in alfalfa and grain classified him as a pest. Many were killed for coyote or wolf bait during the war against predators. Their low ebb was at nearly the same time as the whitetail deer's. In a way the antelope was even more vulnerable than the deer, since concealment is not one of his tricks. Theodore Roosevelt and his friends hunted pronghorns with hounds and horses.

The pronghorn has always depended upon speed, and although he is a difficult, and often long-range target, he is available for another try—and another. A whitetail hunter who might slip through the woods for days to secure a single shot could lie on a prairie ridge and fire dozens of times at antelope. Although he might cripple frequently, persistence would nearly always get his game, and if he did not score today there would be more chances tomorrow. It was a practice that continued in modern hunting, some riflemen simply waiting until game was moved by others, and often firing at absurdly long distances. At any rate, the pronghorn needed protection in the early twentieth century, when drought complicated other problems; waterhole snipers were especially effective during dry weather, and at the same time the range vegetation suffered.

The lowest point was reached some time in the twenties. Hunting was finally closed and the population multiplied from less than 30,000 animals to about 400,000 today. From today's number the pronghorn will probably recede, for it is loss of range rather than hunting which now governs the runner's fate. On much pronghorn territory are new dust clouds marking the heavy machinery that tears up the sage for wheat or rye. In other sections the sage has been poisoned to make way for grass.

Pronghorns' preferred forage is disputed. It appears that much of the sagebrush area of the West was formerly grass, and that the sage took over when grass was overgrazed by buffalo or livestock. So the popular concept that the pronghorn actually prefers sagebrush or rabbit brush to other growth may be erroneous. He has adapted to a situation through the years and his use of forbs and grass, as well as other plants besides sage, indicates that sage may be a substitute. Biologists feel there is little competition between cattle and antelope, somewhat more between antelope and sheep. Pronghorns are seldom guilty of overgrazing, partly because they move over wide areas. Their role as wanderers of the wastelands may be involuntary; perhaps they would prefer the fertile lands now fenced and cultivated.

In a mountainous area of southern Canada in the nineteen-thirties a packtrain made its way slowly and laboriously

Passenger pigeons traveled
in huge flocks, making easy targets for
shotgunners. They were not game
in a sporting sense, and vanished when
commercial killing broke up
their immense roosting and nesting sites.

Coyote hunts rodents and rabbits
in open country. Upland-game hunters study
terrain around high-country
sheep sheds where Hungarian partridge often
headquarter in fall. Grain
and weed seeds abound near buildings,
and birds use shelter in
stormy weather. Hun is prime example of
adaptation to changing habitat.

toward bighorn sheep. It would be gone a month, and the men who paid for it had made a long railway journey before the horses were saddled. They were trophy hunters, experienced with big game, and they had chosen their outfitter with care. It was a complicated business and they had studied maps and pored over record books to learn that part of the high mountains which had the exact combination of habitat to produce the wide-based curling horns they sought. There were rugged peaks in the mountains, but they would hunt on broad-shouldered, grassy bulges that sloped down to aspen-filled draws and were traced by cold rivulets from melting snow. Below them would be dark expanses of conifers that folded into brushy canyons of down timber, and the trails would be those made by game, often difficult for the wide packs and plodding horses.

At first the packtrain moved easily, leather creaking and hooves clopping steadily, with an occasional ringing contact of metal shoe against stone. Farther up the slopes there were complaining grunts from the horses, the tearing crack of dead branches caught in the packs, and goading commands by the guides and wranglers. Several days from the railroad they made a base camp of wall tents near a spring which was enlarged by careful digging and shored up by stones. Then they began inspection of the surrounding mountains through a series of short trips on horseback, sweeping each likely slope with their binoculars, and often crawling to high lookouts where they were careful lest the game should sight them.

They saw sheep, most of them of no interest to trophy hunters, but they located distant groups of rams, indistinct through the shimmering mirage of great distance, and they planned extended approaches that would require spike camps, possibly more than a day's ride from their base. They began separate hunts, each sportsman with a guide, and camped where night found them. The final stages of the quest were executed on foot, stalks that might last for an entire day, and usually for specific rams believed to carry heads that could meet their requirements.

In ram country there were some nearly vertical cliffs that appeared from a distance to be scarred by intersecting cracks that faded away where the precipices merged into more gentle slopes. They were not cracks, but the narrow trails of sheep leading from bedding area to grazing plot, and to broken country where harried rams could disappear from the rifleman's sights in headlong leaps. Across grassy openings the bighorn might run in what appeared to be a tight and rather choppy stride, but when sure footing gave way to narrow chasms or precarious slide rock the wild sheep became a leaping gymnast.

In southern Alberta in the thirties there were not many serious trophy hunters. Most sportsmen knew the white Dall sheep of Alaska and the Stone sheep of British Columbia only by report, and the desert bighorn of the Southwest was hardly noted as a separate variety by many of them. The few riflemen who sought wild sheep in America then were little hazard to the populations. It had been a long time since sheep had moved upward and away from civilization, so they were no longer killed in large quantity for miners' or ranchers' tables. But another ordeal of the mountain monarchs was yet to come.

The "grand slam" of the sheep hunter means collection of one of each of the four North American varieties: Dall, Stone, bighorn, and desert bighorn. It is the desert bighorn that has become most difficult to collect, a sheep with limited and fragile habitat,

living in the southwestern United States and in Mexico. There is no longer unlimited licensing of desert-sheep hunters, and the number of legal permits, acquired by lot, is extremely small, both in the United States and in Mexico. Only the oldest rams are now harvested legally, no serious loss to the nearly extinct type of sheep which once fed railroad builders and cattle drovers. However, the sudden desirability of a mounted desert-sheep head has led to some illegal shooting, despite the jealous guardianship of game officials, and the killing of a single prime member of a clan is a bitter loss to those who have worked so hard to save the sheep.

Mountain sheep cannot be controlled like elk or deer, and some bands have dwindled for no known reason, probably because their range has been reduced. They have been susceptible to domestic sheep diseases. The hope of the bighorn and desert bighorn is in the small colonies that have been reintroduced to range where they once died out or were killed. Not all of the colonies are prospering, but there is less danger of disaster now that the game is somewhat scattered. There is still sheep hunting in the western mountains, although it has become a matter of special permits in most areas south of Canada.

It was after World War II that wilderness big game suddenly became available, partly because of national prosperity, and partly because of advances in transportation and roads. The pack trip that had taken a month in the thirties was now streamlined to accommodate the tight schedules of busy sportsmen. A businessman could leave his office in New York on Friday evening and be camped high in the Canadian Rockies by Sunday night. Enterprising outfitters were prepared to meet hunters at the larger airports with light airplanes, and sometimes they could be flown directly to base camps, miles from highways. Hunts became much shorter, and the bush pilot was an expert game spotter.

As a convenience, the bush plane was invaluable, but in some cases it became a hunting tool that gave the hunter an unfair advantage, and many laws have been written in the interests of fair chase. There were some areas, especially in Alaska, where the pilot could sight Dall sheep from the air and then land his plane on a nearby landing strip which had been cleared previously. (Guides might have a great many such strips in good game country, often with rough camps already established.) Within a few hours the hunter might have his trophy and be headed homeward, satisfied with the result of his expenditures, and leaving the guide free to fly in another customer. Moose, generally found at lower altitudes, were hunted on brief expeditions from lakes that accommodated float planes. The light plane attracted more controversy through its use in polar-bear hunting, although disagreement as to the white bear's status continues in the nineteen-seventies.

Most laws regarding use of aircraft in guiding and outfitting have been based on a length of time required between the plane's landing and the hunter's collecting the game, but regulations have been difficult to interpret and enforce.

The Rocky Mountain goat lives mainly among spires and crags rather than on the high, grassy pastures used by mountain sheep. Being less desired as a trophy, and not much in demand as food, it changed its location less when civilization reached the valleys. There are still huntable quantities of goats in the western states and Canada, and trapping and transplanting have been successful on some ranges.

The elk faced the firing lines at the borders of preserves and in some cases died on overcrowded range. In the nineteen-fifties it retreated from the snarling efficiency of powered vehicles built to invade the wilderness. In some places the ruts of hunters' vehicles started washes that changed whole mountainsides. Primitive areas were designated, machinery outlawed, and miles of privately owned elk country were closed to the public. Vehicle regulations multiplied on public lands.

But the animals had learned ways of surviving among hunters. At first many of the wapiti had been plains animals. Then they were confined to mountainous country and their migrations blocked. Finally, like the bobwhite quail, the elk turned to heavy cover when hard pushed.

On the first days of the hunting season the creamy bulls could be sighted and stalked in open parks and on grassy ridges, but after the first shots they moved to the tangles of windfallen timber in steep-walled canyons. There, in chilled half-light, the hunter seeks them. He moves slowly and looks for antlers that match dead branches. He finds fresh tracks where he has heard nothing move, and he waits long for a sliding shadow or a snapping twig. Several hundred pounds of elk have learned to move in silence, and heavy antlers are deftly tilted to travel narrow game trails. The animal that once was butchered on the plains has changed its ways.

⌐

The game preserve is an essential part of modern management, giving an opportunity for a species to multiply in safety, but the regulation of preserve herds is essential. In most cases the preserve objective is to keep an inviolate nucleus sufficient to populate a surrounding territory that is open to hunting. It is when the preserve populations become too large that managers run afoul of preservationists who resent any harvest within the sanctuary. Sentimental pressures by antihunting groups have increased with the number of preserves, and frustrated managers have sometimes been forced to cancel special hunts that would stabilize the population. Nature strives toward a balance, but the true one is seldom achieved. It is especially difficult in the artificiality of a preserve, and a hundred years of warfare against predators have made the situation worse. The same sort of imbalance has been aggravated when hunters who were used to buck-only regulations have resisted the necessity for shooting doe deer as herds became too large.

Waterfowl preserves have encountered a special problem of their own in recent years. Normal migration routes have been changed by the resting areas which attract thousands of ducks and geese unwilling to leave the comforts man has provided for them. Some migrations have thus been cut off from southern states, while shooting has improved on borders of refuges in the Midwest. Now there is a threat of overcrowding and the possibility of disease.

Waterfowl management was mainly a matter of generous bag limits until the twenties and thirties. Then the flights dwindled because natural drought dried up the nesting area of the northern United States and southern Canada, and because systematic drainage and damming destroyed thousands of acres of wetlands. More recently there has been frantic Government and private effort at acquiring marshes for waterfowl use; at the same time Government funds have been used to subsidize drainage for agricultural purposes. It is the deep-water ducks that suffer through the pollution of rivers. Grain-eating puddle ducks or dabblers fare better because they can feed on farmland.

Without help from organized conservationists, the raccoon spread its range, almost as rapidly as the coyote moved to new ground. It was wel-

comed by hound users, who loved the night-bugling of a pack more than a kill, but there were no explanations for much of the increase. In some of the prairie states the raccoon took to the creek beds that had been growing to larger trees for a hundred years since the prairie fires ended. The raccoon—living somewhere between prized game animals and harrassed predators like the fox—had never been hated by varmint hunters. Some of its return was keyed to a lack of interest in its fur, which once had been a trappers' mainstay.

The cougar or puma of the West, the same animal as the East's panther, was making an unusual change in status by 1970. It had neared extinction through the remorseless pursuit of bounty hunters and Government control, and suddenly the bounties were removed in most areas. In some states it became a recognized game animal and its pursuit controlled. In others it was completely protected. Its numbers are few, but it is widely scattered in primitive areas, a condition that has led to revival of other endangered species.

The wild turkey, a subject of long and frustrating study, has made a spectacular comeback. By 1970 it was found in great numbers in the West, East, and Southeast, while flocks were introduced to some western and midwestern areas where they were unknown a hundred years ago. Part of the turkey's success was due to new understanding of turkey diseases. Mingling with tame strains had formerly caused destruction when wild birds contracted afflictions for which they had no resistance, diseases that might readily be shaken off by tame birds with a background of natural immunity.

Some of the heaviest game required special attention, long after mule and whitetail deer were again available in plenty. The moose was subject to limited hunting in the West; in Maine it never returned in large numbers, although eastern Canada retained successful hunting seasons. The Alaskan moose, largest of the tribe, continued to prosper although endangered for a time by trophy seekers in bush planes. It was found in much of western Canada. Farther south along the Rockies, most moose hunting was by permit, and game managers found the world's largest deer had a disturbing tendency to tameness in some sections.

Government agencies which have guided the fortunes of wildlife during the twentieth century have been supported by a number of influential laymen's groups, some of which existed before any potent Government forces became active.

The Boone & Crockett Club was organized in 1887 with Theodore Roosevelt as a guiding hand. It was a group of prominent big-game hunters dedicated to the welfare of wildlife, and it exerted enormous political influence. Hunters who have little knowledge of its contributions to game conservation know the Club through its record-keeping of American big game. It began ranking outstanding trophies in 1929. Its first book of records was printed in 1932, using a system of measurements now nationally accepted. Updated books are issued at regular intervals.

The National Audubon Society appeared in 1902, as an organization of local groups. The New York Society was the first, beginning in 1887. The Izaak Walton League of America was founded in 1922 and began with private purchases of land for elk refuge. The American Wildlife Federation, an association of conservation groups, came in the thirties, as did the American Wildlife Institute.

Ducks Unlimited has long been champion of the waterfowl. Private support of ducks and geese began with the American Wild Fowlers Society in the twenties, later becoming the More Game Birds in America Foundation, and reorganizing as Ducks Unlimited in 1937, the same year in which the Pittman-Robertson Act set up a program of taxation on hunting equipment and ammunition with the proceeds to be used in game conservation. Ducks Unlimited, using private funds, has been able to preserve and construct waterfowl breeding areas in Canada, projects that could not be handled by U.S. Government funds. Their surveys of duck and goose conditions are widely accepted additions to Federal estimates. A Federal licensing program for waterfowl began with the Migratory Bird Hunting Stamp Act in 1934, a time when duck and goose shooting seemed near an end. Now game protection organizations number in the hundreds.

⌐

The beginning of the twentieth century found hunters turning to smokeless powder. Damascus, or "twist," shotgun barrels could not accommodate its higher pressures, but the beauty of Damascus designs was such that for a time the modern fluid-steel barrels were sometimes colored to imitate it. Automatic and pump shotguns began to take the place of doubles, a takeover that reached its peak shortly after World War II.

Military cartridges were the basis for much of the high-powered rifle ammunition, and the .30/06 became a standard for game from whitetail deer to the largest brown bears. When such cartridges came into sporting use the rifleman discovered the principles of shock as applied to bullets, and the manufacture of projectiles became complex, with various weights and jacket strengths applying to different kinds of hunting. Bolt-actioned rifles gained popularity because they could bring out the accuracy of the new ammunition, and telescopic sights were used to employ it to best effort.

For a time there was a continual search for higher and higher velocity in big-game cartridges, and some proponents felt bullet weight was unimportant if enough speed could be generated, while other firearms experts clung to the heavy bullet with its deep penetration. Eventually, nearly all American big-game cartridges were compromises, although varmint cartridges went to such high speeds that many varmint rifles suffered rapid barrel erosion. Through all of this, the .30/30, although moderate in velocity, retained its popularity in lever-actioned rifles.

The .280 Ross cartridge, originated by Sir Charles Ross in Canada in 1910, was a forerunner of the high-velocity cartridges to come, but the rifle built for it was inferior and its popularity was short. Savage's .250/3000, designed by Charles Newton, is still widely used as a deer cartridge and was one of the most successful of the early high-speed, light-bullet cartridges.

Hand loading, responsible for a great many "wildcat" cartridges that later became factory loadings, was in the doldrums from the time of efficient factory cartridges until after World War II, when it enjoyed a rapid growth, both for rifle and shotgun users. Leading ammunition manufacturers, after holding a dim view of hand loading for many years, began to encourage it with a wide selection of components.

With game limits reduced, many hunters handicapped themselves deliberately with primitive weapons, and archery grew rapidly after 1945. Muzzle-loading and black-powder breech-loading guns enjoyed popularity with numerous clubs, shooters using both antique arms and currently built replicas. Special seasons for primitive weapons became a part of game management, and there is now a growing doctrine that the hunt is more important than the kill.

9. New Gam

e for Old

Man fosters change, for better or worse, and one way he does it is to take live birds and animals with him wherever he goes. Many creatures have been transplanted for no better reason than man's endless passion for toying with nature. Often, a hunter moving to new country is nostalgic for the game he has hunted before and so he wants to see it introduced to his present location. A few transplanted species have been worthwhile additions in their new homes; many more, however, have failed or turned to nuisances, and some have become downright plagues upon the land.

America now has the ring-necked pheasant, a bird so firmly established that it is almost as much American as Asiatic. Generations of hunters in the United States have considered it the leading upland game bird, and thousands of gunners have no interest in other game, saving their vacations and ammunition for pheasant season each year. Some of them do not even know the names of native game living with the pheasant, and hope that interlopers such as sharp-tailed grouse or prairie chicken will not interfere with the gaudy one's welfare.

After numerous attempts at introduction, the Chinese pheasant found its first secure American home in the Willamette Valley of Oregon, arriving there in 1881. It had gone to Europe from Asia centuries before, and was long established in Britain. There are many kinds of Asiatic pheasants, but those that first accepted American grain and willows were truly from China, and most hunters call all pheasants "Chinese." There was an open season on them only ten years from their first successful introduction. After 1920 the Dakotas and Nebraska became the best-known part of pheasant country. Now the birds are spread over most of the adjoining states north of Oklahoma, and there are successful pockets of them farther south.

The pheasant's intelligence is legendary and it differs from other game birds in its quick changes from barnyard fowl to difficult game, the individual bird seeming to sense when it is being hunted. It is hunted in as many ways as there are different types of terrain and is a constant surprise to pheasant gunners. In midwestern cornfields, pheasants are sometimes driven up in flocks over standing gunners; at other times the pheasant hunt requires the finesse of whitetail deer stalking. True experts study terrain and vegetation, estimating the routes of birds that would rather walk than fly, and planning approaches that less astute hunters would never consider.

Along a river of the Northwest the willows are thick beneath tall cottonwoods. The rosebushes cling to man and dog, and small creeks and sloughs are filled with cattails, some of them broken over and matted. The ground beneath the cattails is boggy, and when the surface of the shallow water freezes slightly it becomes impassable for any but the most resolute dog. In the thick weeds between strands of cattails, the midday hunters flounder and sweat, hoping to fly an occasional pheasant that becomes cornered against a small open place. The bag is small—if *any* birds are killed.

Late in the day most of the hunters are gone, having kicked the half-frozen mud from their burdened boots and mopped weed seeds and sand from their guns. Their dogs, bedraggled and exhausted, looked for help in their jumps to the dog boxes of pickup trucks and station wagons. Several hunts have ended and another begins.

The newly arrived hunters have studied the river and fields, and they are slow in starting.

Opening pages: Asiatic pheasant
is outstanding example of imported game that
has found a home in game
fields of America. The "chink" is resident of
grain country and nearby cover,
providing hunting through most northern states.
Methods vary from drives
in Nebraska cornfields to pointer work along
river bottoms of Far West.

It has been some time since the last shot from the river bottom and the new hunters stop at a haystack to survey the situation. Half a mile from the river bed are wheatfields, alternating strips of tan stubble with black cultivated strips of ground between, and between the wheat stubble and the river brush are cropped hayfields, broken by narrow irrigation ditches with their streaks of tall grass and weeds.

The important feature is a single wide ditch, well grown up with willows and strips of cattails. It runs unbroken from the wheatfields to the river, offering unseen passage to any bird that goes from safe resting areas to the open feeding grounds. The two hunters at the haystack know that pheasants will take that route to the wheatfields before dusk, for pheasants feed then.

They begin the hunt at the river end of the ditch, knowing that the birds already have begun to move. Most of the ground has thawed during the day and it begins to freeze slightly as evening comes on, but not before pheasant tracks have been made in the mud and in patches of old snow.

The dog is a slow worker, an old Brittany who has played the game many times before, and he pushes about in the grass and weeds of the ditch. In its wider places the cover is thirty yards across and it must be explored thoroughly. Several times the dog trots along on the downwind side of the strip, enjoying the easy going of the level hayfield, and prospecting for scents from unseen parts of the narrow hunting area. He shows no inclination to leave the ditch's edges and there is a hunter on each side, walking very slowly. Now and then one of the gunners wades into the thicker grass with his attention on the area ahead, but for the first two hundred yards there is no visible sign of birds. They have

been there, for the dog alternates high-headed wind searching with ground sniffing, and the men read his actions through long experience. They talk freely across the ditch and they step on dry weed stalks wherever convenient so there will be no doubt of their location and progress.

At one point the dog stops on the downwind side of the ditch, pointing tentatively. Then he hurries forward, and the hunters know he is scenting moving birds, but they do not yet expect a shot. Once a few blades of grass move on the ditch's edge. At another spot the ditch makes a sharp bend and a cock pheasant takes a shortcut. He comes out of the cover and travels for a few yards in the open, taking long strides with his head thrust forward, late sun flashing from the red and blue of his brilliant plumage, his long tail straight back. He sees a hunter and runs faster. When he turns back to disappear in the weeds, his wings cup slightly to retain his balance.

The strip of cover bulges into a patch of willows and bushes bordering a clump of cattails, and the dog points solidly, a blob of white and orange a little below the hunters. One of them hurries into the weeds and approaches the dog, hoping the birds will hold long enough to be flushed. Just ahead of the dog's quivering nose, the hunter stops and kicks about violently, but the bird has moved again and the old Brittany looks up apologetically and starts ahead once more. A bird flushes with staccato cackles and a broken squawk. It flails at the weeds and goes almost straight up for ten feet, but it comes from a spot the shooter had not expected and it has reached the top of its climb before he can face it. It turns in the air and goes back toward the river with noisy wings, momentarily concealed from the nearest man by high willows. It is the other hunter who

*Artist depicts dog flushing
flock of pheasants. Asiatic birds have been
tried in a variety of forms
as biologists attempted to fit them into
various climates and habitat
over entire United States. Many types of birds
have interbred until their exact
ancestry is uncertain. Proud dog brings in
America's favorite upland prize.*

*Cock pheasant is slow riser
but flusters novice gunners with cackling
and noisy wings. Birds are fast
runners, preferring legs to wings in most
escapes. Mowing machine is
enemy of nesting hens in alfalfa during
summer haying. Ideal habitat
has access to weeds, brush, and grain. Bird
refuses to adapt to Southwest.*

fires from the open. The bird dives with its wings folded and thuds against the ground, trailing a thin streak of feathers. The shot brings another flush, this one too far forward, and a third bird skims the hayfield to the rear, having doubled back and made its escape. The hunt is resumed in the direction of the wheatfields. There are other birds to be bagged, but many have slipped to the rear and are running back to the river bottom. The same hunt can be made again in a few days.

❧

Ideal pheasant habitat contains grain with heavy concealment nearby. The popularity of the bird is partly dependent upon its table qualities, for it has the least wild taste of any upland game, and it is large enough to seem worthwhile for hunters who feel a successful hunt must result in a family dinner. The beauty of a mature cock appeals to those who are less impressed by the muted tans and grays of other game birds. And the pheasant can be an easy mark, especially when it rises at close range, since it lacks acceleration. Its cackles can unnerve shooters, but they add to the drama of a flush.

When the bird was first established in the northern United States, hunters and game managers believed that the basics of grain and concealment were the only requirements. There were repeated introductions in the Southeast, where bobwhite quail and turkey needed reinforcement. Those plantings never succeeded, even when made with Asiatic varieties accustomed to hot weather. In some hot sections of the Southwest they prospered. Pheasant breeding has become an important game-farm effort, and for many years there have been introductions of birds that appear much different from the classic ringneck. Now it is believed that soil composition is basic in pheasant welfare; for some reason, few good populations exist where the earth has not been subject to considerable freezing. Lime is deemed important, but the ideal soil constitution is still mysterious.

Pheasants suffer from the same hazards as other upland birds. Drought can reduce vegetation, wet weather during nesting season can reduce the hatch, and heavy snow for long periods can cause winter kill. Although hardy for short periods of cold, the pheasant can be killed by persistent blizzard conditions. Nesting hens often choose alfalfa fields where they are slain by mowing machines. But prolonged reduction of pheasant populations is most frequently a result of changing land uses, often from grain to pasture. In marginal areas, where the breeding population is insufficient, put-and-take planting is a frequent device, an expensive and wasteful practice that makes roast pheasant the most expensive item on the hunter's menu. It has been learned that birds should be put out only a few days before season opening. If too much time is given, they may disappear completely, generally traveling rapidly on the ground in search of habitat that suits them better. Sometimes they take resident birds with them. Most of the put-and-take birds are cocks, hens being retained to continue the hopeless task of propagating birds where conditions will not accept them.

Many of the pen-reared birds are never harvested. There is always loss to predators, and many pheasants simply wander away from the guns to perish during the winter. On the other hand, it is not desirable for an excess of the planted cocks to survive, for they can overcrowd the range in spring and reduce the hatch survival of native birds. In pheasant reproduction, only one male is needed for several hens.

Hunters and farmers are inclined to blame overshooting or predators for scarcity of birds, and there is a call for reduced hunting whenever a

change in crops drives the pheasant population down. Such pressure, in overwhelming and concrete form, confronted the game officials of the nineteen-sixties. Alarmed by thinning pheasant numbers, farmers banded together and threatened to close large areas of land to all hunting unless game managers accepted their dictates as to pheasant seasons and bag limits. Since most pheasant habitat is in farmland, conservation officials have been forced to bow to these pressures in many instances, sometimes against their judgment as to the effect on the larger ecological picture. Although farmers are not necessarily wrong in their assessment of game conditions, too often they are mistaken in holding to the ancient theory that if game is left alone, it will multiply. In most cover, two pheasants at winter's end will likely mean only two pheasants in another year, regardless of hunting results; stockpiling seldom occurs. Yet, the principle that game tends to find its own level has not yet been sold to the public.

Where a pheasant population is healthy, it is often desirable to shoot hens to some extent, but there is much resistance to this, as there has been to

Covey of Hungarian partridge flies across western fields. Birds prefer a combination of grain and cover. Lower left: Sharp-tailed grouse gather to perform mating ritual. Pointers hold as grouse flushes. Hun hides in grass. Sage grouse cock struts on his booming ground in one of nature's most dramatic mating demonstrations.

doe shooting from deer hunters. Those who do not believe in shooting hen pheasants have some argument in marginal areas where gunners do not expect to get a limit. If one hen and two cocks are allowed in a limit (a common regulation), it is likely that the shooter will collect more hens because usually they are easier to find. Thus he might make several trips and kill a hen on each, while the more difficult cocks escape, and it is conceivable that the ratio of cocks to hens could be exactly the opposite of what is desirable.

While the brilliant Asiatic pheasant cackled his brassy way across America, the gray partridge arrived unheralded and merged with the grassy edges of the wheatfields. Fifty years after he had occupied his new home, many of the farmers who owned the land he occupied were uncertain as to his name, and in the West many of them simply called the birds "little chickens." Most professional game managers called them Hungarian partridge, or Huns. That is their most popular name in America today, but their identity is confused enough that the scientific name of *Perdix perdix* must frequently be relied on.

By about 1910 the Hun had occupied much of the Northwest, though which introductions were successful was never known. Since the birds are small and easily transported, they were released repeatedly by early settlers of the East, but none of the early introductions endured. Probably the most successful of the western plantings was in southern Canada, and it is popularly believed that the northern United States was occupied by birds from Canada after plantings south of the border had died out. Their home is near big-game country for the most part, and they drew little attention from outdoorsmen more interested in elk. The Hun seemed trivial, and at the time of his arrival there were few bird dogs to hunt it. Walking up Huns is a difficult task, for they usually are thinly spread and their flights unpredictable. Even today, the birds attract little hunting pressure, and game managers are uncertain as to their scarcity or plenty. They live in a broad land, and their fluctuations go unrecorded.

The Hun coveys are family groups in September, when many shooting seasons open, and young birds of the year are obviously smaller than adults. Late in the fall the birds are of about the same size, and some family groups will have merged. At first the wild-flushing Hun was unsatisfactory for users of pointing dogs. But the gray-partridge hunter is a specialist in the same sense that a ruffed-grouse lover is a specialist, and the distant flush with a covey of birds wheeling against the autumn sky is part of the game for him, even though he cannot shoot at that distance. He marks the descent with care and plods toward the new landing spot. And if such a performance will cause a classic pointer to learn strange habits, the owner does not complain, for he is not hunting a bird that holds predictably in classic fashion.

In Europe, the partridge has long been the subject of drives, with beaters pushing birds to a row of shooters, and many European gunners who have shot partridges for years are surprised to learn of their performances on the wheatfields and high grazing land of the West. In America, in normal years, the Hun spreads thinly and a single covey's territory will embrace a square mile, or more if forage is scanty. It was many years before American hunters developed methods for the bird (they are characteristically slow to accept new game).

Early hunters of the Hun found its patterns mystifying. The birds show a strong tendency

to alight on the near side of a hill, then walk over the top to hold a position just beyond the crest. Hun hunters learned that habit quickly, but there were times when big coveys of mature birds seemed to evaporate, and no eager pointer or jogging athlete could find them or put them into the air. There would be a leisurely flush, a little out of range, and the flock would take a definite turn and make a sloping landing that seemed to indicate the direction it intended to run. Then, unseen, the birds would reverse their course and run back through the cover in the direction they had flown from, skirting perilously close to the hunters and dogs in the process. The frustrated hunter might give up the quest, only to see the birds fly from an area he had not searched at all. More

frequently, he never saw them again.

This unpredictability is still largely the rule. There are days when the Huns watch a hunting party from a hillcrest in grazing country, staying in short grass that gives a view of all surroundings. The hunter may see them fly repeatedly at a distance from which he can barely identify them. He may hunt diligently in a creek bottom where he has found birds before. When he finds nothing he ascends surrounding hills. His dog makes game on a shorn crest—game that is no longer there—and the hunter knows he has been under surveillance all along.

On another day, when he is sure all Huns are sitting on bare hills watching tired hunters,

he walks the curve of a little creek bed where the grass is a bit higher than on the surrounding ground, and a dozen gray and reddish-brown birds go up about his feet with alarmed chirping. He is surprised and probably misses what is a rare and easy chance, and he wonders how his dog overlooked the spot.

On the other hand, coveys have been known to hold together through as many as eight consecutive flushes. Often the pattern of flight is circular and the covey may finally return to the exact spot it left the first time. The same covey may do this again on another day, and the hunter takes satisfaction in predicting the performance.

There have been occasional years when partridge appeared in bumper crops and spread to unlikely places. Generally, their residence is near grainfields, or on the slopes near them, but in the best years they sometimes have been found on snowy mountainsides, above 8,000 feet, with a full view of sunny valleys and grainfields. Some would fly down for morning and evening feeding. Others were so far away from grain that they may never have visited it. (In Europe, on the contrary, the Hun has always been associated with grain.)

There have been Huns on arid pastureland, miles from grainfields, living along the small creeks and arroyos. Others have stayed in sagebrush hills. They have favored abandoned farm buildings and sheep sheds. They have been found together with valley quail, pheasants, chukars, sharp-tailed grouse, prairie chickens, and sage grouse. They have proved adaptable in many respects, but they have lived widely scattered in most years.

The gray partridge has become more and more important to conservationists, not because of being so widely hunted, but because it seems capable of survival without the attention lavished on pheasants and of promising game for the future. By the nineteen-seventies state game biologists were engaged in studying this self-sufficient immigrant, a study that had been postponed for more than half a century.

Although there has been much bungling in the introduction of new animals and birds, the experience with the chukar partridge from India has been almost entirely successful. The bird accepts a rugged home that other game birds don't want, and that man has found little use for. If other game eventually disappears under the pressure of human enterprises, the chukar could well be the last wild observer to stand on a high stone spire and cackle down at a valley crawling with people and their machinery.

It is the most recent of successful additions to the game list. Not until 1947 did hunters begin to stumble across talus slides in pursuit of the derisive calls that came from ever farther ahead and higher up. Several years later they began to develop hunting methods, none of which has ever been easy.

The chukar is one of a number of red-legged partridges, and the birds that took to the Great Basin wastelands came from Asia, probably most of them from India. There have been many plantings, however, and crossbreeding has confused the origins. The first recorded immigrants arrived in 1893, but most of them disappeared. In those early days of game study, the usual policy was to plant them in conditions improved over those found in the bird's native strongholds, "improved" by human standards, that is. It seemed logical that a resident of desert and sun-baked cliffs would be happier to live among fertile grainfields and lush valleys, and those who went to great effort and expense to import

*Chukar partridge is one of
most successful introductions to American
hunting, for it has adopted lands
of little value for anything else. After it
failed to survive in fertile
grainfields of the Midwest, it took happily
to arid mountains of the
West. It is hunted on rocky slopes by hunters
willing to climb and crawl.*

chukars did not consider that arid hills might be what the chukar really wanted.

An old hunter recalls early encounters with chukars, handsome gray- and black-barred birds with flashing red legs and brilliant crimson beaks, that trotted in confusion along midwestern fencerows. The gunner, who had come out for quail, was disappointed to find that the big birds, weighing more than a pound, did not want to fly and had no plan for concealment. Some of those first birds had lived in wicker cages in Asia. The chukar can be domesticated, and some have been used as fighting cocks. When they are employed as game-preserve targets they can be too tame, dusting busily before expectant dogs and shooters, and running in circles about trees or rocks when pursued by amazed pointers. In such surroundings they are victims of an unfamiliar environment to which they cannot adapt.

In the sparsely covered mountains of the semidesert lands of Nevada or eastern Washington, the chukar is more at home. There the introduced birds disappeared, reappearing much later in healthy colonies. The typical chukar home is on mountains, but not far from water. In dry weather there are great flocks along the skimpy watercourses and the hunter is likely to see them as disturbed shadows, running swiftly upward toward rimrocks, far above the creeks. They are heard and seen on nearly inaccessible cliffs above western impoundments. It is nearly an inviolate rule that the chukar runs up and flies down, and many hunts are panting pursuit of a quarry the hunter cannot outrun. If he can force the game to the very top of a slope, it may fly almost over his head on the way back down. It plunges past him, driven both by powerful wings and by gravity, as he stumbles in his haste to achieve a reasonable shooting position and get off a shot.

An extended chukar hunt in new territory is likely to involve days of unproductive scouting before birds can be approached, and the experienced hunter is patient as he plays a game of calculated moves. He may scale a mountain and rest on a rock outcropping to listen to the calls about him. From the valleys the calls are even more confusing. The chukar is noted for noisy communication with his kind, but there are days when the canyons are silent. When the calls come, they are cackles in which the bird seems to repeat its name, and sometimes it is impossible to tell the exact direction or distance as wind sweeps the sounds about the crags and echoes multiply them. From his high post the hunter may look across a canyon to a wall of rimrock with slides and patches of grass and sage. He hears calls from several points of the rock, and other cackles rise from below it, so he tries to see a route by which he can reach the birds.

The Barbary sheep, or aoudad,
is still on probation in America, but has
provided sport on many
preserves. Chief question about such game is
its possible competition with
native animals, so game managers must move
slowly with introductions.
Russian hogs have been sporty game for hound
men and interbreed with feral natives.

If he has chosen his lookout wisely, there may be calls from his side of the canyon; if they are near his altitude, or slightly below, he prepares for the climax of his labors. Usually, he is at the top of his ridge; he moves along it, walking slowly with frequent stops, and frequently seeing signs of the coyotes which also use such places to survey the land.

Suddenly the nearby cackling ceases and he knows he is near the game. He listens carefully, making sure that all of the calls come from across the canyon, not close at hand. Before him is a chain of rimrocks and jutting boulders, and he watches the rocks far ahead as well as those at his feet, for he may see a chukar lookout, standing erect with extended neck, outlined against the sky. He may hear a murmur of restless birds, or even the delicate patter of their feet on the rocks.

When the birds go, they hurtle down the slope with squealing calls. The first few feet of the flight are likely to be downward, as the birds gain velocity. Then they can be expected to head almost straight out and turn down into power dives. The critical point is when they tip downward. It is easy to misjudge and shoot over them. If the hunter anticipates the dive he may shoot low. He may make his shot looking almost directly past his feet, seeing only the top side of the bird as it levels off. Those that escape become specks in the misty canyon. If nothing breaks his view he will see their course change a little as they prepare to land, and might even catch the last few feet of fluttering descent. Now he expects them to start back upward afoot and he will try to meet them. He must guess how near the top they will come before they hide. If the canyon is a small one, he is in excellent position. But if it has taken hours of climbing to reach his place, he hesitates to lose hard-gained altitude, and may decide to find a new covey.

It is a chukar hunter's rule that most of the birds on a given day will be found at roughly the same height, sometimes well below the crest.

The chukar's staple diet is cheatgrass, an exotic that has flourished in overgrazed sections. It is in seedling stage during winter; in early summer it dries up and becomes a fire hazard. Cheatgrass is despised by stockmen but beloved by chukars, and it has its counterpart in Asia. However, grain is also welcomed by chukars as long as suitable refuge is available in the form of steep slopes, tumbled rocks, and stone caves for shelter from severe weather.

There are days and places when chukars can be hunted much like Hungarian partridge or prairie chicken. Some steep slopes lead upward to broad flats of grass and sagebrush, and the flocks will work well away from their refuge. Then it is possible to find them with pointing dogs. Often they hold well and the hunter has the advantage of knowing they will nearly always fly back toward the cliffs. A similar situation arises when grainfields are separated by deep erosions, such as are found in eastern Washington. The wheatfield may be almost flat, but its edge breaks into a precipitous plunge to a thread of creek far below. Chukars live on the slope but feed in the stubble above in morning and evening. Thoughtful hunters, using dogs, can trace the edge of the steep ravine, staying just a little below the top and out of sight of the grainfield. When the dog shows sign of birds over the edge, the gunner can move up a few yards and cut them off when they fly toward safety. If he hunts the grainfield in plain view, the birds are likely to flush wild.

Chukars are most often seen near water, and many observers do not know that they spend less time there than on the slopes. When there has been heavy rain, the birds may abandon the streams and scat-

ter in rough country wherever rock pockets make cups for water.

Of all American upland game, none seems to fluctuate in numbers so wildly as the chukar. Flocks will seem to evaporate in poor years, only to return as suddenly as they faded. Hunters are now becoming accustomed to reports of an annual seventy-percent natural mortality among upland birds, yet such a figure is much too conservative for application to chukars in poor years.

Washington, Oregon, Nevada, and Idaho have led in chukar harvests, but they are found in most western states and parts of Canada, as well as in the Hawaiian Islands.

There have been many failures with new game. One of the most spectacular was that of the coturnix quail, a natural resident of both Europe and Asia. Somewhat smaller than the bobwhite, the coturnix multiplies rapidly and can be pen-raised in large numbers without great effort. The bird was tried on many earlier occasions, only to disappear, but the strongest effort on its behalf was in the late nineteen-fifties, when state game departments released them by the hundreds of thousands in the Midwest, East, and South. It appeared the coturnix would not be a serious competitor of the bobwhite as far as feeding was concerned, and sportsmen felt it would hold well for pointing dogs.

But the coturnix is migratory in both Asia and Europe, making long seasonal trips between warm and cold climates. It apparently flew far away from release sites, and few of the released birds were ever seen again. Some biologists were relieved that the experiment failed, despite its expense, for they had feared that the prolific aliens might change their ways in a new land and become a liability. There were good precedents for this apprehension. The English sparrow, imported as early as the eighteen-fifties, spread over North America to become a pest. It was the object of some hunting, and was even served in a few restaurants. It also was used as targets for shooting matches. Nevertheless, there are few Americans today who would not wish to see the English sparrow leave. The starling, like the sparrow, was imported from Europe and spread to all fifty states, beginning early in the twentieth century. Both species originally had been expected to destroy harmful insects.

Not all introductions have been planned. Before the Civil War, Arabian camels were used by the United States Army, as well as by some civilians on the Texas plains, and when their owners were through with them they were simply turned loose; many escaped. Even years later, individual beasts appeared near water holes in the dry lands, and great cloven tracks were disturbing to travelers who did not know the camel story.

The camels have long since disappeared. Another beast of burden has become controversial, however, as a competitor and physical enemy of native game. It is the common burro, patient helpmeet that has carried loads for thousands of prospectors and performed other important tasks in the Southwest. Many of them have escaped or been turned out to make their own way in the desert, and numbers of them still live there, competing with the native bighorn sheep for food and water in a shrinking habitat. Despite their comical appearance and reputation for faithful service, burros gone wild are sharp-hooved assassins at times, reported to attack livestock and drive wild sheep away from waterholes. When California hunters undertook to thin out the animals in the nineteen-fifties, they aroused a storm of disapproval from persons who believed the burro had a right to the desert—a right acquired by more than a hundred years of residence. The problem has not been resolved.

In western North Carolina a game preserve was established in 1912, and among the animals stocked were Russian hogs, noted for great size, long tusks, and evil temper. They were even more dangerous than the domestic American hog gone wild. Russian hogs which escaped that confinement have evidently crossed with the American feral hogs, or razorbacks, and ever since the combination has been game for packs of hounds in the Great Smokies of Tennessee and North Carolina. The Russian boar has been introduced elsewhere as well, and colonies have been hunted recently in California, but in most cases the "wild hog" is simply a well-adapted truant from an American farm.

At question in most introductions is whether the new resident in new surroundings will be game or not. Only after the bison had begun to come back under full protection and management did biologists realize that it had never been a game animal in the sense that the whitetail deer or mountain sheep are. When the numbers were sufficient for hunting, most such "hunts" were simple matters of selecting an animal from a herd and executing it. Even the use of primitive weapons did not make modern buffalo hunting adventurous. Most hunters are content to view the shaggy beasts in a preserve.

America's Southwest has a climate and terrain very similar to parts of Africa. Before 1950 many African animals had been lodged there under preserve conditions. It is now possible for a hunter to pursue a variety of exotic game for a fee there and in other states, but whether the imports could be worthwhile if added to public lands is questionable. The Barbary sheep, or aoudad, a 300-pound native of northern Africa, has been living in the wild in Texas and New Mexico for some time, and limited hunts have been successful, but the days of careless plantings are almost over and it will be years before definite decisions about the Barbary sheep can be made. Chief among the managers' worries is the likelihood that an exotic with African background might carry disease to native game, and compete in habitat with the struggling bighorn.

Within the country there is a traffic of native birds and animals being transplanted by amateurs. This is carried on less guardedly than similar attempts made with species from abroad, and usually is done by well-meaning persons. Still, they rarely understand the problems of transplanting, and may cause considerable upset to an ecology by their introductions.

Even well-managed introductions are often only experiments. There has been a great deal of trading between game departments. The whitetail deer has been moved from states where it grows to large size in the hope that it would improve herds of small deer. In most cases the newcomers were simply absorbed and their progeny soon appeared in the same form as the original residents. When western pronghorns were recently introduced to the weed and palmetto flats of central Florida, they simply disappeared. Mountain sheep, goats, antelope, and elk, however, have been introduced freely, often with success, though most of these plantings have been made where the habitat is already known to be suitable, and newcomers usually occupy range previously used by the same species.

Man has engineered shifts in the world's wildlife, and will continue to do so, but even the most studious biologists lose more often than they win in attempts at introduction.

10. Man and

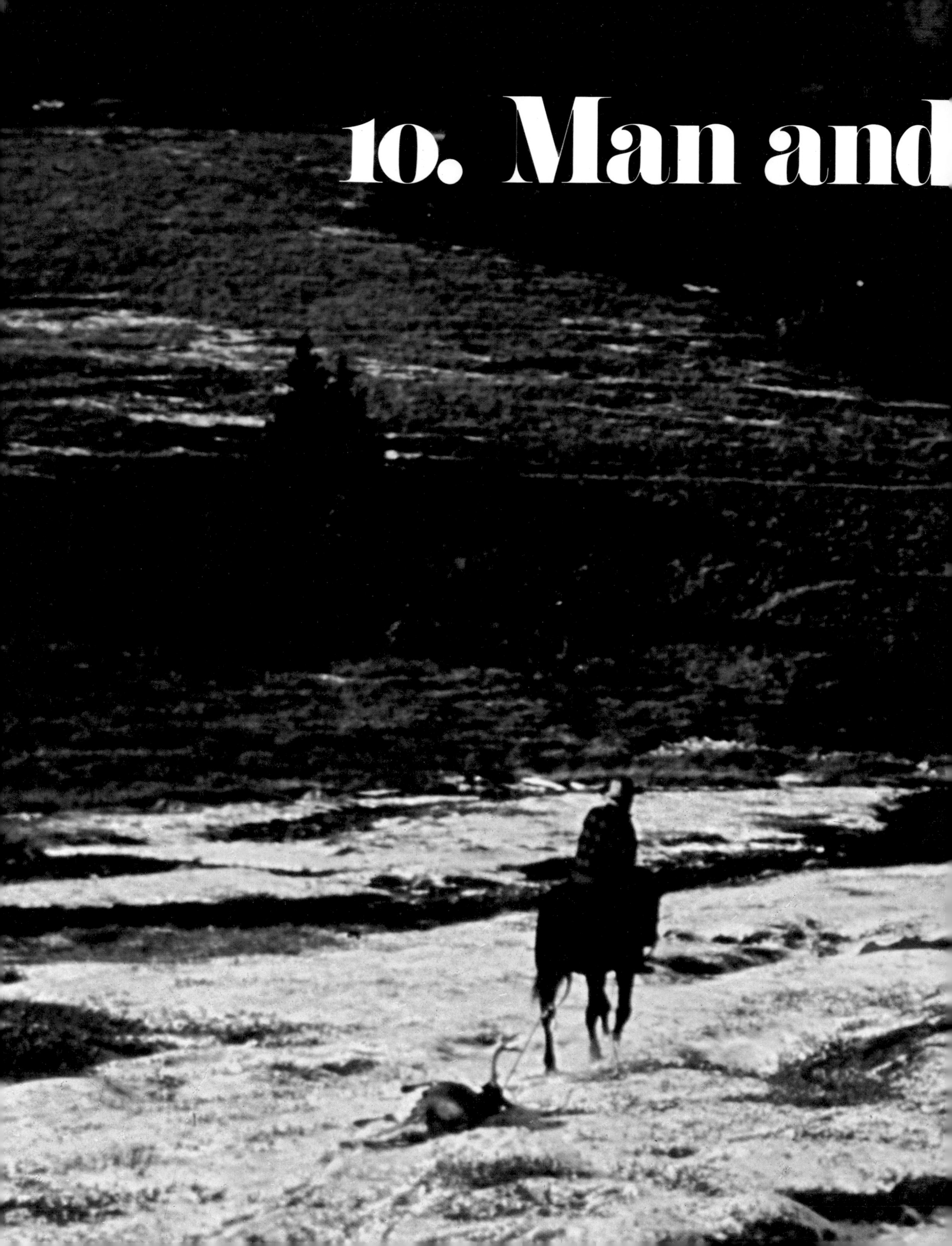

the Balance

ost American game animals have multiplied since their low ebb of seventy years ago. Given sufficient habitat, game managers have been able to find solutions for most shortages. There are exceptions, however, species that simply cannot cope with civilization. The mountain sheep and the grizzly bear, for example, are true wilderness creatures. The sheep is restricted to greatly reduced range, ravaged by excessive domestic grazing, and overhunted in many areas. The grizzly, pursued relentlessly for one hundred and fifty years, is not wanted in large numbers, for it is the one animal that can be a physical danger to man and his livestock. The puma and the wolf are dangerous to livestock when found in quantity, but neither is numerous today, and they are now being protected.

These species aside, American game animals are now crowding the shrinking areas allotted to them. The hunters have multiplied, too, and although they have sponsored the return of the game they now face a shortage of space in which to hunt it. Space has been lost not only through the spread of civilization but also through the growing tendency toward preservationism.

With an aroused public accepting ecology as a sacred trust, there has been a turn toward a philosophy that, in its extreme, allows no human change in nature. People of strong antihunting sentiment are deaf to the valid arguments that exist for the necessity of trimming numbers of many species. They believe that the hunt is basically cruel, and that the killing of a bird or animal is a crime against nature. And their prejudice against hunters is not mitigated by the fact that the restoration of the species over the past seventy years has been accomplished largely through the efforts of hunters' organizations.

Most of the troubles being experienced by American hunters, like most of the improvements in hunting conditions, developed gradually, but one problem—the closing of territory to hunting—made itself felt in a surprisingly short time. It was a process by which a minor annoyance might grow into an insurmountable obstacle within a year or two. In a given area, a single landowner would close his property, whether for good or poor reasons, and his neighbors would receive the brunt of those hunters who were now denied land they had been using for years. A second and a third closing then would make it impossible for other property owners to keep their land open as the number of the hunters descending upon them snowballed. Eventually, an entire area would be closed. Whether the original closing was justified or not, the final posters would be put up out of necessity. The effect is just as if the landowners had made their decision at a mass meeting. Reasons for closing can range from a simple matter of excessive hunting pressure to cases of vandalism or thievery, but in the eyes of the farmer the hunters are reduced to the lowest possible denominator, the invader who does the most harm.

At the same time that private lands were being closed to hunting, public lands, too, were becoming more difficult of access. For many years hunters have often seen National Forests, dedicated in spirit to multiple use, become a source of immense wealth to mining, lumbering, and ranching interests. The localized habitat destruction caused by mining is plainly visible. The lumber industry has affected forests adversely in many ways (some of them were actually beneficial to hunting). Cattle and sheep ranchers have used the forest for low-cost grazing, paying a fraction of the cost they would for private-land use. Overgrazing has

*Opening pages: A Canadian hunter
drags in venison through snowy valley. Hounds
used in earlier cougar hunt
follow second horseman. Mule deer and cougar
have long lived together,
with great cat performing as regulator of
deer herds. Below: Mountain
goats feed on steep slopes where wind clears
snow from scant vegetation.*

*Game trails cut high slopes
of grizzly country. True wilderness is
choice of unpredictable bruins in
mountain and coastal regions. Wide-antlered
moose walks shores of
lakes and bogs, feeding on willows and
underwater plants. Grizzly
is busy fisherman during salmon run and
reaches greatest size along coast.*

Varmint shooters use precision rifles and high-powered scopes for wary woodchucks. Too many hunters can be a nuisance to farmers; ideal is to keep population at satisfactory level for both rifleman and grower. Golden eagle, hunted for years as harmful predator, was protected when conservationists opposed killing.

damaged some game habitat to the point where many years of careful management are needed to return it to productivity. Even with grazing quotas that in many cases are too large, it has been standard practice to exceed the quota. If a rancher was caught with too many cattle or sheep the penalty would be minor and ineffective.

Hunters observed the misuses of National Forests and made occasional complaints, but it was not until they found themselves denied access to public land that their complaints became really vocal. This happened as landowners fenced the hunter away from publicly owned land to which he had as much right as the rancher—perhaps more, since his taxes paid for upkeep of the National Forest and he enjoyed no grazing rights. The rancher or farmer living on the edge of the Forest did not want the bother of hunters on the ground where his livestock grazed, so he simply locked his gates or put fences up across country roads. For their part, the hunters had little legal recourse for gaining admission, short of condemnation proceedings. This is a difficult sort of action in livestock country; juries of ranchers are not likely to take kindly to such affairs.

In many cases where access to a National Forest is allowed, the hunter is also confronted by the problem of getting his big-game animal out through roadless country. With vehicular traffic restricted due to the land erosion it causes, a pack string is the only answer—and this is an expensive solution.

Where they are not flatly excluded, hunting parties may be charged a fee for crossing private land to hunt in National Forest land. Some hunters pay it willingly, feeling the extra cost will reduce hunter competition. However a nonresident of a big-game state must often assume still other costs in hunting the National Forests, and this has engendered some bitterness. Ownership of the game is public, and the game within a National Forest is under the control of the state within which the forest is located. The nonresident hunter must pay a high license fee to the state in which he is to hunt, usually roughly ten to fifteen times the cost of a resident

*Horses have aided big-game hunters
in most wilderness areas. Bighorn sheep is
usually sought with packtrain.
Binoculars are important part of hunt in
West, where game is located
at long ranges. Pack horses (lower left)
carry out moose antlers through
mountain valley. Hunters of an earlier day
rest their game-loaded horses.*

license. As an instance, in 1972, Montana's regular big-game license for nonresidents cost $151, not including special permits. But Montana law prohibited a nonresident hunter from hunting big game in most areas unless accompanied by a resident license holder. Thus, for the privilege of hunting in a National Forest he helped to support, the nonresident had to pay $151 plus the expenses of being accompanied by a Montana resident with a hunting license. This procedure is very good for the guiding business. The nonresident fees, of course, pay the lion's share of the state's game-management costs. Other western states present similar licensing problems, generally obstructionist toward the nonresident.

In the East, leased hunting is a rapidly growing approach. Sometimes it is done through a club, or by an individual paying for rights to large sections, or sometimes through payment of fee to a landlord who prefers not to bother with individual hunting requests and allows the lessee to handle posting and policing. Leasing has been a traditional process with duck-hunting privileges for a century. It is increasingly prevalent with upland game coverts today, to the despair of the occasional hunter who has no place to go.

The public shooting preserve is an institution where the individual can hunt for a fee, usually with most equipment furnished. Pheasant, bobwhite quail, and mallard ducks are most frequently used as game, although some commercial grounds offer turkeys, chukar partridge and exotic big game. Sometimes the operator can produce wild game as well as pen-raised birds. Without the preserve there would be no hunting in localities where private owners have closed their property. Some professional game men maintain that leased land and the hunting preserve are the sport of the future. Without them, they say, there will be no hunting at all.

Preserve operation is a new science. It is not simply a matter of raising birds in pens, and it is far more complex than a live shoot of trapped domestic pigeons. The best preserves offer a hunting experience as near as possible to one involving wild game, sometimes within the confines of a very small perimeter and on the very edge of metropolitan areas. Preserve birds can vary from "barnyard birds" that are easy marks to game that is indistinguishable from wild natives. The better preserves pen-raise their birds with a minimum of human contact.

The quail plantation is a southern tradition that remains strong in the twentieth century. It is devoted to the propagation of bobwhite quail, and hunting is still done in the grand manner, often with shooting wagons drawn by matched mules. Pointers and setters ride in the box, several braces of them to be sure that fresh dogs are on the ground at all times. Dogs are followed by handlers mounted on Tennessee walking horses, and once a covey is found, flushed, and shot, the job of retrieving is done by a specialist, a Labrador or spaniel who rides in a special place on the wagon, while the pointers are off again in search of another covey.

The plantation does not provide public hunting, and it may close off land to hunters who cannot afford the privilege, but it has served as a quail laboratory where the bird has been thoroughly studied and where land has been managed to produce the best in quail numbers and shooting. If a field trail is held on such property, the pointing of a hundred coveys in a day is not unusual. Here the bobwhite is raised as a successful crop—good news to hunters.

The mourning dove is controversial as game. Many states regard it as a songbird to the despair of hunters who consider it a target of special

Cold-weather big-game hunter is both camouflaged and protected by his white parka. Arctic temperatures complicate hunting methods and care of equipment. Eskimos have taught sportsmen the ways of primitive life. Much large game is hunted in bad weather, and polar bear or caribou are seldom taken without hardship.

qualifications. It is listed as a migratory resource and is subject to Federal regulation. Dove hunting seasons are set—as is the case with waterfowl—within a nationally established framework of shooting time. Individual states are privileged to maintain closed seasons if desired. Nevertheless the dove hunters are everywhere opposed by preservationist and nonhunting groups.

Dove hunting requires only shotgun and ammunition, and dove hunts are often community affairs in which the gunners cooperate on likely fields, pass shooting birds that cross the field or circle in looking for feeding sites. Thus, a small area can accommodate a dozen shooters or more, making large hunting areas unnecessary, and the occasional shooter is able to participate with little effort and expense. Some game departments have established sponsored shoots in which hunters pay a small fee or none at all, and hunt on an area leased or "borrowed" by the state agency. Shooting days are spaced to avoid undue pressure.

The dove is prolific, with a high rate of natural mortality in the best years, evidently regardless of hunting pressure. It has long been a popular game bird, but its importance has increased and it has shown a remarkable adaptability to civilization.

The white-crowned pigeon is one creature that is endangered by the hunter's gun, and its status is a modification of that of the passenger pigeon. Like the passenger pigeon, it is addicted to slavish flight routes, especially during the nesting period, and will fly almost straight at an anchored boat where hunters can shoot it in large numbers. Limits are destructively high. It lives, breeds, and makes its short migrations in the Caribbean and was once plentiful in the Florida Keys, where there is no shooting today. However, it nests on islands, where game laws are sketchy.

*Marshes and bogs play large
part in hunting. Sportsmen with muzzle-loaders
(below) explore a marsh with their
dogs. Shorebirds and rail live where
water meets land. Green-winged
teal (right) is elusive target. Hunters in
blind point at black
duck, prize of the Atlantic flyway and one
of the most intelligent birds.*

European hunting dogs have made
great advances with American sportsmen as
twentieth century nears
close. The weimaraners shown on point are
general-purpose hunters and
have been trained for furred and feathered
game. Europe was source of most
early American hunting dogs as well, but
these are new "foreign" dogs.

Although it can be a difficult mark at times, the white-crowned pigeon loses its evasive tactics when engrossed in feeding or nest tending. Thousands have been killed on their unbending flight routes, often very near the water between islands. A frequent aftermath of the shooting is that the young are left to starve. The flocks do not approach those of the passenger pigeon in size, but there are many disturbing parallels between the white-crowned and the now-extinct passenger pigeon.

The white-winged dove, similar to the mourning dove, is a popular target in the Southwest, where the supply fluctuates greatly. In Central America the kill is sometimes enormous, with shooters from the United States in the role of tourist hunters. But, as yet, the whitewing is not suffering as the white-crowned pigeon has.

In upland game management, the concept of natural mortality as the major factor in bird supplies has been the subject of a difficult educational program by Government agencies. Experiments have shown that habitat rather than hunting pressure is the major factor in the over-all population; the hunter's kill comes from a surplus of birds that probably would be regulated otherwise by natural hazards.

In Arizona, hunting pressure was tested on Gambel's and scaled quail. One area was closed to all hunting for several years while similar adjoining terrain was left open. After the experimental period both areas were tested as to hunter success, with the conclusion that hunting pressure had no influence on the number of birds present.

Season lengths and bag limits are minimal as regulating factors in many instances. In exceptionally good years the hunters are busy and many secure limit bags. When the bird population is down, hunting pressure fades rapidly after the season's opening and the kill dwindles to a fraction of that made in good years. Even modest limits are not taken. The adjustment may work by the same principle as that of wild predator-game relationships, in which the number of predators is automatically reduced during a scarcity of game. Man as a predator also adjusts, and even the legal restrictions he places on himself in the interests of the game may be considered as part of the process.

There are some problems for which the hunter can blame no one but himself, such as lead poisoning of ducks and geese. For generations hunters have fired their lead shot over the same marshes, the expended pellets sinking to the bottom by the ton. Where the bottom is firm, shot is easily picked up by feeding waterfowl. Inside the bird and in contact with digestive juices, it becomes poisonous, and the death toll has grown to epidemic proportions with further shooting destined to compound the hazard. Ducks have died by the thousands, and conservation organizations are now insistent that some other form of shot be used.

Lead shot is still the basis for virtually all effective shotgun ammunition. It is heavy enough to carry up well when fired, and it is soft enough not to damage steel barrels. Gold and silver would be satisfactory substitutes, except that they are prohibitively expensive. The firearms industry turned to soft steel in a series of experiments. The disadvantages were that some pellets were destructive to shotgun barrels and too light to maintain velocity over long ranges. When existing shotgun barrels were tested it was learned that even the best grade guns sometimes had barrels of relatively soft steel that could not withstand abrasive contact with steel shot. Gun authorities sadly contemplated the neces-

sity for short-range shooting on waterfowl and feared that much crippling would result, since duck and goose hunters are noted for long-range attempts and are not likely to change their habits. It seems improbable that a nonpoisonous shot can be developed in the near future that will shoot as well as lead. All of the prospective substitutes are expensive.

In equipment, the gunner of the seventies has shown a tendency toward fine weapons, partly because the value of fine guns has been increasing for many years; those purchased fifty years ago are generally worth much more today. Most of the fine custom rifles being made worldwide are the products of a few famous American builders, some of whom are bringing to rifles the meticulous attention that once made English shotguns the standard of the world. Actions and barrels come from both Europe and America.

Japan, too, has gone far in firearms manufacture, and some of the largest American firms are relying on the Orient for certain models in their lines, especially double-barrel shotguns. Labor costs in Great Britain have hampered the shotgun production there and raised the prices enormously; while there is always a ready market for the limited output of very expensive guns, many British sportsmen of modest means are turning to imported weapons. Italian and Spanish companies are producing a large share of the medium- to high-priced guns, and other European countries are doing the same on a somewhat smaller scale. German and Belgian factories produce many guns that appear on the market with American trademarks.

European hunting dogs have invaded the American scene increasingly in recent years. The German shorthaired pointer, the Vizsla from Hun-

Pheasant is colorful target
as it flushes from cornfield; variety of
dogs is used by upland hunters
below. Following pages: Hunter crouches for
better chance at woodcock in
thicket, aided by English pointers, as bird
flies "for the light."
Good woodcock hunters become experts at
choosing route of flushed bird.

gary, and the French pointing Brittany are now well known. The weimaraner is a general-purpose hunter from Germany which has made a strong impression in America since the end of World War II. The German wirehaired pointer has a unique appearance for Americans accustomed to sleek pointers and setters. Another wirehair, the pointing griffon from Holland and France, has a reputation for close-working efficiency. Although overshadowed by the English springer spaniel, a long-time American favorite, several European flushing dogs are now in use in this country. The Irish water spaniel has never achieved the prominence of the Labrador, but it has a long American history. Most of these European dogs have earned their places both as hunters and as family pets.

Domestic animals can also be predators of wild game. This is a frequently overlooked factor in areas where civilization has absorbed wildlife habitat. Uncontrolled packs of feral dogs, a byproduct of suburbia, are multiplying as nocturnal killers of game and nongame species and are becoming an underworld of the wild. Many of them enter the wild as unwanted pets abandoned by sentimental owners who cannot face the destruction of an animal, but who give no thought to its becoming a predator or starving. Feral cats, although not inclined to pack activity, have propagated on the fringes between civilization and game country, and have taken a toll of game birds as well as songbirds. The wild cats and dogs are bolstered by part-time killers, pets that sleep by the fire by day and join the marauders by night. Most former pets have superior intelligence and there are no satisfactory methods for destroying them. The very fact that they are able to exist in the wild designates them as resourceful survivors. There is also a

Quail are mainstays of native game-bird hunting. Bobwhites (left) are chief quarry of Southeast. Hunter with Brittany spaniel is shooting harlequin quail near Mexican border. Some species are found only in wild country, but bobwhite can be raised as a farm crop. Its management is highly advanced in both field and pen.

tendency for wild dogs to breed to an efficient size; they are among the most adaptable of creatures. Such an animal might have been the beginning of Australia's dingo, said to have sprung from domestic strains, and now as much a part of the wild scene as the wolf or hyena. Thus, man had added a predator. The wild hog is another, although its depredations are less spectacular and less harmful; also, it can be game.

Predation, an essential part of game welfare, requires regulation, especially when man himself is the predator. Some self-regulation has occurred in the killing of woodchucks and rockchucks. Expert users of long-range precision rifles have tempered their sport so that the woodchuck will not become too scarce, nor be present in such numbers as to provoke the farmer to begin a program of extermination.

There is danger to the golden eagle from human predation. For years it was considered vermin in much of its range, mainly because it is dangerous to newborn domestic lambs, partly because it is a minor predator of mountain sheep. Then its cause was taken up by conservationists who began an energetic drive to enforce laws for the prevention of eagle killing. It remains to be seen how much impact this will have on the individual rancher who suffers some personal loss. Those who believe there are too many eagles will probably continue to shoot them, if necessary, to protect their animals.

American game is much more plentiful than it was seventy years ago. It now appears that a crop of wildlife can be provided as long as there is room for it, but the high point has been reached. The prime concern of the conservationist is no longer to suppress hunting activity; the fight now is for space and habitat.

America has its own tradition of hunting, a kind of tradition shared only by the newer nations of the world. It is the tradition of the "hunters of Kentucky," of the mountain men, and of the buffalo killers. It is based upon independence and the belief that game is public property.

But the spirit of the buckskin rifleman and the commercial gunner of 1880 must now be tempered due to lack of hunting room. There will be more and more hunters using less and less land. Already in the United States there are parallels to the European concept, in which game is owned privately and harvested by a privileged few—the few with the means to manage the game. American sportsmen face greater management if they are not to lose their sport entirely. There will remain some hunting for all, but limits will be reduced and the state maps of hunting areas will grow in complexity as managers divide their land into ever smaller districts to give closer attention to local conditions. Those hunters imbued with the independent spirit of the frontiersman will be unhappy to find themselves subject to increasingly restrictive regulations.

Game laws are essential and many hunters obey them meticulously. But the outdoor idealist who thinks that the laws on the books will completely regulate the harvest is not reckoning with the carefree attitude of many Americans toward misdemeanors. A nation that played happy games with Prohibition and considers traffic laws a sort of hide-and-seek is slow to take wildlife management seriously.

In this matter the judiciary has a shameful record, with many judges handling cases as if game violations were beneath the court's dignity, the equivalent perhaps of apple stealing by small boys. When a judge smiles at such misdemeanors, the conser-

onvoi funèbre du chasseur. ——— Des Yägers Leichenzug.

THE HUNTER'S FUNERAL.

vation officer loses both prestige and authority. In the future, game laws must carry heavier penalties, and judges must impose them. A popular attitude toward wildlife conservation will one day make such penalties acceptable.

Progress is slowed by the fact that there is much disagreement over procedures among people who are working toward the betterment of the wildlife situation. Opinions are constantly becoming obsolete in light of modern research, and the professional biologist's task is frequently complicated by opposition from the very conservationists he tries to help. The process of game management is now one of education as much as field procedure. The hunter may observe game during hunting seasons, but ignore developments for the remainder of the year. Yet he forms strong opinions on the basis of this incomplete data and tends to be skeptical of the findings of controlled scientific studies. Government agencies are constantly faced with public ignorance, yet when biologists make a mistake it is remembered for years.

Government scientists, particularly in many state agencies, work in the shadow of pressures exerted through political channels. Hundreds of dedicated biologists have found themselves unemployed because their findings did not agree with the interests of hunters or developers who had political influence. Such a situation can arise when biologists try to protect a predatory species, such as the cougar, from the ire of hunters who compete with it for game. In some cases the opposing viewpoints are based on apparently worthy reasons, as when game-rich marshes are drained to afford relief from flood dangers, to destroy mosquitoes, to provide new land for farming, housing, or industrial development. It was well into the twentieth century before anyone ap-

preciated the value of the true wetlands as incubators of wildfowl and certain forms of ocean life, and therefore as deserving to exist for their own sake. In the future, where the interests of man and game are opposed, man must win, but the issues cannot be dealt with in simplistic terms. The need to balance conflicting interests is a stumbling block to the dedicated professional, who must sometimes remain too conservative for the game's good and occasionally must place public relations before achievement.

There is a saying in management circles that there are three phases to a management program: First, the old and undesirable procedures must be abandoned without arousing public opposition (as in the case of the large-scale quail hatcheries). Second, there must be energetic work on worthwhile projects currently accepted by the public. Third, there must be constant education toward procedures so advanced the public does not yet accept them. This is game management in the twentieth century.

A sensible harvest of game depends increasingly on the hunter's knowledge of his quarry. When old trophy rams are to be pruned from desert-sheep herds, the shooter must be trained to recognize legal game. No fine or jail sentence can replace a young and virile male shot by mistake. In preparation for such hunts some states require the hunter to undergo a test of his observation, actually viewing from a distance horns installed on dummy specimens.

The waterfowler's sport is increasingly complicated by the necessity for recognition of species under hunting conditions, and the recognition booklet is part of his kit. He needs to know those species that are completely protected. In addition, he may be hunting according to a point system that has been adopted in many areas—a plan which allows the hunter generous limits of those ducks in good supply and restricts him sharply on those that are scarce. His day's limit is figured as a mathematical sum, a mallard drake counting for very few points and a hen mallard adding heavily to his total. Thus, the recognition expert can bring in a much heavier legal bag than the uninformed shooter who sees all ducks as similar outlines.

Federal control of migratory species has been accepted gratefully by most state wildlife professionals, because it divides the harvest more fairly in most cases. The usual procedure is to give each state a time frame within which it can set a season to please its hunters while limiting the total number of shooting days. Before such regulation existed it was possible for a migratory species whose over-all population was low to be overkilled while concentrated in a given area. It was difficult to convince hunters they were shooting game that was in short supply nationally. Federal regulations have reduced the possibility of irresponsible local political action toward game.

The Federal laws have sometimes produced unexpected complications, as with the measures that protected alligators from skin hunting, one of the last of the large-profit poaching enterprises. It is of little use for one state to prohibit alligator killing if a neighboring state permits sale of the hides. It is impossible to police the swamps where alligators live, and smuggling hides across a state line is simple. Federal controls seemed the only way to deal with the poachers who were rapidly destroying the alligators and getting high prices for the hides. But not long after Federal closures went into effect there appeared an overabundance of alligators in a small sector of Louisiana, and the state declared an open season in a limited area. The ramifications were far-reaching and a complex system of control was necessary to prevent illegal operations. There was never any doubt that Louisiana had more than enough alligators, yet the harvesting activity could have put the entire protective structure in danger of collapse. It is one example of the complexity of management.

Enlightened conservationists are better equipped and organized than ever before, and their contribution is great. However, they are fighting against the extinction of some species that may in the end prove unable to survive in tomorrow's world. An example is the whooping crane, guarded from a distance and observed as closely as modern technology permits; the few dozen living whoopers may be the most expensive birds the world has ever known. The loss of a single one to a vandal or a natural predator receives national attention, whereas the loss of a thousand mallards to a drainage project may go unreported. Since extinction and replacement are part of nature, there are some who argue that the money and effort spent on preserving this species could be better deployed.

Scientific knowledge of game moves on, but some things are learned too late in the game. It is only recently that "worthless" swamps were understood to be the most essential cradles of wildlife. It is only recently that the Arctic tundra, with all its proof against cold, was revealed as fragile before the works of man. The lesson in these discoveries is that man must make "progressive" changes with careful circumspection, lest irreplaceable natural assets be lost in the process.

The long rifleman is with us in spirit, and that spirit is part of hunting's proud heritage. But we now understand that we must replace what we take if hunting is to have any future. No longer can we move across new ranges as the game disappears.

Canny whitetail deer is king
of American big game, living close to city
or farm, and capable of hiding
in brush patches or fencerows. Whitetail has
overpopulated some sections
in return from low point about 1910. Doe
hunts were needed to regulate
numbers, but once sportsmen adapted to buck
hunting they refused does.

Bibliography

Allen, Durward L., *Pheasants in North America*.
Harrisburg, Pa., Stackpole Books, 1956.

Baity, Elizabeth Chesley, *America Before Man*.
New York, The Viking Press, 1953.

Bandi, Hans Georg, *Eskimo Prehistory*.
Seattle, University of Washington Press, 1969.

Bogardus, Adam H., *Field, Cover & Trap Shooting*.
New York, Forest & Stream Publishing Co., 1891.

Boone & Crockett Club, *North American Big Game*.
Pittsburgh, Pa., Boone & Crockett Club, 1971.

Brander, Michael, *Hunting & Shooting*.
New York, G. P. Putnam's Sons, 1971.

Brennan, Louis A., *American Dawn*.
New York, Macmillan Company, 1970.

Burke, Edmund, *The History of Archery*.
New York, William Morrow & Co., 1959.

Bushnell, G. H. S., *The First Americans*.
New York, McGraw-Hill Book Co., 1968.

Camp, Raymond R., ed., *The Hunter's Encyclopedia*.
Harrisburg, Pa., The Telegraph Press, 1948.

Ceram, C. W., *The First American*.
New York, Harcourt Brace Jovanovich, Inc., 1971.

Christensen, Glen C., *The Chukar Partridge*.
Reno, Bulletin, Nevada Dept. of Fish & Game, 1970.

Clark, Grahame, *The Stone Age Hunters*.
New York, McGraw-Hill Book Co., 1967.

Cleland, Robert Glass, *This Reckless Breed of Men*.
New York, Alfred A. Knopf, 1963.

Coon, Carleton S., *The Hunting Peoples*.
Boston, Atlantic Monthly Press, Little, Brown & Co., 1971.

Dobie, J. Frank, *The Voice of the Coyote*.
University of Nebraska Press, 1961.

Dodge, Col. Richard Irving, *The Plains of the Great West*.
New York, Archer House, Inc., 1959.

Elman, Robert, and Peterson, H. L., *The Great Guns*.
New York, Ridge Press, Grosset & Dunlap, 1971.

Farb, Peter, *Man's Rise to Civilization As Shown by the Indians of
North America from Primeval Times to the Coming of the Industrial
State*. New York, E. P. Dutton & Co., 1968.

Gard, Wayne, *The Great Buffalo Hunt*.
New York, Alfred A. Knopf, 1960.

Haines, Francis, *The Buffalo*.
New York, Thomas Y. Crowell Co., 1970.

Hewitt, Oliver H., ed., *The Wild Turkey and Its Management*.
Deposit, N.Y., Valley Offset, Inc., The Wildlife Society, 1967.

Hibben, Frank C., *Hunting American Bears*.
Philadelphia, J. P. Lippincott Co., 1945.

Hinman, Bob, *The Golden Age of Shotgunning*.
New York, Winchester Press, 1971.

Interior, Dept. of, *Waterfowl Tomorrow*.
Washington, D.C., U.S. Government Printing Office, 1964.

Johnson, Peter H., *Parker, America's Finest Shotguns*.
New York, Bonanza Books, 1961.

Kaufman, Henry J., *The Pennsylvania-Kentucky Rifle*.
Harrisburg, Pa., Stackpole Books, 1960.

Knight, Charles R., *Prehistoric Man, the Great Adventurer*.
New York, Appleton-Century-Crofts, Inc., 1949.

Kortright, Francis H., *The Ducks, Geese and Swans of North America*.
Harrisburg, Pa., Stackpole Books & Wildlife Management
Institute, 1942.

Laycock, George, *The Alien Animals*.
Garden City, N.Y., The National History Press, 1966.

Madson, John, Library of game books for the conservation department
of Olin Mathieson Chemical Corp.

McAtee, W. L., *The Ring-Necked Pheasant*.
Washington, D.C., American Wildlife Institute, 1945.

Matthiessen, Peter, *Wildlife in America*.
New York, The Viking Press, 1959.

Morison, Samuel Eliot, *The European Discovery of America*.
New York, Oxford University Press, 1971.

National Geographic Society, *Wild Animals of North America*.
Chicago, The Lakeside Press, 1960.

Outdoor Life, *The Story of American Hunting and Firearms*.
New York, McGraw-Hill Book Co., 1959.

Patterson, Robert L., *The Sage Grouse in Wyoming*.
Denver, Sage Books, Inc., 1952.

Peterson, Harold L., *Pageant of the Gun*.
Garden City, N.Y., Doubleday & Co., Inc., 1967.

Point, Father Nicolas, *Wilderness Kingdom*.
New York, Holt, Rinehart & Winston, 1967.

Pope, Saxton T., *A Study of Bows and Arrows*.
University of California, 1923.

Rosene, Walter, *The Bobwhite Quail*.
New Brunswick, N. J., Rutgers University Press, 1969.

Russell, Carl P., *Guns on the Early Frontiers*.
New York, Bonanza Books, 1957.

Sandoz, Mari, *The Battle of the Little Bighorn*.
Philadelphia, J. P. Lippincott Co., 1966.

Simak, Clifford D., *Trilobite, Dinosaur and Man*.
New York, St. Martin's Press, 1966.

Taylor, Walter O., ed., *The Deer of North America*.
Harrisburg, Pa., Stackpole Books & Wildlife Institute, 1956.

Trefethen, James B., *Crusade for Wildlife*. Harrisburg, Pa.,
Stackpole Books and Boone & Crockett Club, 1961.

Wisler, Clark, *Indians of the United States*.
Garden City, N. Y., Doubleday & Co., Inc., 1966.

Woolner, Frank, *Grouse and Grouse Hunting*.
New York, Crown Publishers, Inc., 1970.

Picture Credits

AMNH—The American Museum of Natural History
BB—Bill Browning
EAB—Edwin A. Bauer
HE—Harry Engels
JVW—Joe Van Wormer

LC—Library of Congress
LLR—Leonard Lee Rue
NYPL—New York Public Library
O'R—J. Barry O'Rourke
TGC—The Granger Collection

Front-cover photograph: Bill Browning
Back-cover photograph: Leonard Lee Rue
Credits read from left to right and from top to bottom.

CHAPTER 1

10-11: Paul Baich. 14: "Prehistoric Men" by J. Augusta and
Z. Burian, AMNH; "Smilodon" by Charles
Knight, AMNH: 15: HE. 16: AMNH (both). 17: "Warren
Mastodon" by Charles Knight, AMNH. 18: EAB. 19:
Florida Department of Natural Resources; "Mode of Chasing Bison
by the Assiniboin" by Peter Rindisbaeher,
West Point Museum. 21: NYPL; "Prehistoric Men" by J. Augusta
and Z. Burian, AMNH. 22: NYPL (both). 23: EAB.

CHAPTER 2

26-27: BB. 30: HE; John Borneman. 31: LLR. 32: "The Moose
Chase" by George de Forest Brush, National Collection of Fine
Arts, Smithsonian Institution. 34-35: BB. 37: NYPL. 38: from
Voyages de la Nouvelle France by Samuel de Champlain,
Rare Book Division, NYPL. 39. EAB.
42: The Museum of the American Indian, Heye Foundation (both).
43: BB; " 'Bridal Veil' Falls," Currier & Ives, LC.
46-47: BB. 49: "Hunting the Buffalo" by W.
W. Rice from drawing by F. O. C. Dudley, LC. 50-51: "Buffalo
Chase in Winter" by George Catlin, National Collection of Fine
Arts, Smithsonian Institution. 51: "The Bison, or Wild Ox of
America" from *American Magazine of Useful Knowledge*, LC; "The
Last of the Buffalo" by Albert Bierstadt, Corcoran Art Gallery.
52: NYPL. 54: "Esquimaux Spearing Seals" from
Appleton's Journal, Culver Pictures. 55: Frederick C. Baldwin.

CHAPTER 3

58-59: O'R. 62: LLR. 63: from *America* by Théodore de Bry, Rare
Book Division, NYPL. 64: "Crudelitas Petri de Calyce erga Indos" by
Théodore de Bry, National Collection of Fine Arts, Smithsonian
Institution. 66: NYPL. 66-67: O'R, Joe Kindig Collection.
67: top two from *The Gun and Its Development* by W. W. Greener.
68: NYPL. 69: TGC; engraving after
Frederic Remington, TGC. 70-71: "Landscape
with Travellers II," Anon., The National Gallery of Canada,
Ottawa. 71: LLR; EAB. 72: engraving after Frederic Remington,
TGC. 74: NYPL. 75: BB. 76: LLR.

CHAPTER 4

78-79: O'R. 82: NYPL. 83: engraving by Alexander Anderson, TGC.
84: NYPL; "Turkey Shoot" by Charles Deas, from the
Collection of Mr. & Mrs. Paul Mellon. 86-87: O'R (both). 89: NYPL.

90-91: O'R (all). 92: NYPL. 94-95: BB. 96-97: NYPL. 98: NYPL;
JVW. 99: EAB; LLR.

CHAPTER 5

102-103: BB. 106-107: BB. 107: "Long Jakes" by W.G. Jackson
from painting by Charles Deas, TGC. 110-111: BB. 114-115: LLR.
115: EAB. 119: EAB; TGC. 122-23: NYPL. 126: TGC;
The Kansas State Historical Society, Topeka. 126-127: NYPL.

CHAPTER 6

130-131: JVW. 134: Currier & Ives, LC. 135: EAB; from
Celebrated Dogs of America by A. Pope, Jr., LC.
137: LLR. 138: LLR. 142: BB. 143: HE. 146: JVW. 149: JVW.

CHAPTER 7

152-153: TGC. 156-157: TGC. 157: NYPL; Gernsheim Collection,
The University of Texas at Austin. 159: EAB. 160-161: TGC.
163: Paul D. McLain; BB; BB; NYPL. 164: TGC. 166: JVW; HE.
167: EAB. 168: Shelburne Museum (all). 170: O'R. 171:
Warren Shepard. 173: NYPL. 174-175: The Adirondack Museum.

CHAPTER 8

178-179: BB. 181: NYPL. 182: EAB (top two); BB. 186-187: JVW.
188-189: Culver Pictures. 191: BB (both). 194-195: O'R.

CHAPTER 9

198-199: LLR. 202-203: "Pheasants and Dogs" by John James Audubon, Racquet & Tennis Club. 203: EAB; LLR. 205: LLR. 206-
207: BB; Saskatchewan Government Photographic Services; Currier
& Ives, LC; BB; JVW. 209: Culver Pictures. 210: BB. 211: JVW.
212: The American Philosophical Library.
213: LLR. 215: BB; Tennessee Game and Fish Commission.

CHAPTER 10

218-219: BB. 221: HE. 222: EAB. 223: EAB; LLR. 224: LLR
(all). 226: EAB; BB; BB. 226-227: "A Halt in the Woods" by
Arthur F. Tait, Racquet & Tennis Club. 229: LLR. 230: "Wood-cock
Shooting," Currier & Ives, LC. 231: LC; Graham Wilson-
Leonard Ruenterprises. 233: LLR. 234: LLR. 235: "Quail Shooting"
by Harry Beard, LC. 236-237: TGC. 238: Currier & Ives, LC;
BB. 240: "The Hunter's Funeral" by M. Limpert, LC.
243: EAB. 246: Currier & Ives, LC.

*The sportsman's way of living
has been depicted in pastoral scenes by
early artists, the full life
shown as including hunting dogs and guns, and
hunters shown as lovers of
nature. The first game regulations were at
instigation of hunters who
believed harvest should be regulated and game
should be saved for posterity.*

Index